GROUP WORK IN THE PRIMARY CLASSROOM

Group work is generally accepted as part of the educational ideology of today's primary classrooms. This theoretical acceptance has not, however, always been matched in practice and the term can mean almost anything from group seating, as a technique of classroom management, to full collaborative learning.

The purpose of this book is to provide teachers and those who train teachers with a set of principles which should enable them to increase the effectiveness of collaborative group work in the primary classroom. After a review of the research already done in the UK and USA on the results of group work and children's reactions to it, the authors use original case study material to analyse the classroom practice of teachers attempting to introduce group work to their children. It sets this practice in the general context of existing theories of teaching and learning and attempts to provide explanations for the failure of some activities and the success of others. The result is a planning framework from which individual teachers can derive policies and activities suitable for the circumstances in their own schools and classrooms. This book should be of value to all who work in primary education.

Professor Maurice Galton is Director of the School of Education, University of Leicester. His research, beginning with the ORACLE project, has embraced all aspects of primary education and he was one of the first university professors to return to the school classroom to acquire recent and relevant teaching experience. His publications include *Inside the Primary Classroom*, and *Curriculum Provision in the Small Primary School*. John Williamson is Head of the School of Teaching Studies at the Curtin University of Technology, Perth, Western Australia.

GROUP WORK IN THE PRIMARY CLASSROOM

*Maurice Galton and
John Williamson*

London and New York

First published 1992
by Routledge
11 New Fetter Lane, London EC4P 4EE

Simultaneously published in the USA and Canada
by Routledge
a division of Routledge, Chapman and Hall, Inc.
29 West 35th Street, New York, NY 10001

© 1992 Maurice Galton and John Williamson

Typeset by LaserScript, Mitcham, Surrey
Printed and bound in Great Britain by
Biddles Ltd, Guildford and King's Lynn

British Library Cataloguing in Publication Data
Galton, Maurice, *1937–*
Group work in the primary classroom.
I. Title II. Williamson, John
372.11020941

ISBN 0–415–03630–5
ISBN 0–415–03631–3 pbk

Library of Congress Cataloging in Publication Data
Galton, Maurice J.
Group work in the primary classroom/Maurice Galton and John
Williamson
p. cm.
Includes bibliographical references and index.
ISBN 0–415–03630–5. – ISBN 0–415–03631–3 (pbk.)
1. Group work in education. 2. Education, Elementary – Great Britain.
3. Education, Elementary – United States. I. Williamson, John. II. Title.
LB1032.G33 1992
372.13'95–dc20 91-28499
CIP

CONTENTS

FIGURES

TABLES

PREFACE

Group Work in the Primary Classroom describes research which has taken place at the School of Education, University of Leicester, since 1980 when the then Social Science Research Council (SSRC) funded a three-year project on the topic. By the end of the three years the project had reached few positive conclusions apart from the fact that motivating children to work collaboratively in groups and managing this activity was extremely difficult. But a fascination with the topic and a conviction that collaborative activity in the primary school was a necessary and valuable experience for all pupils resulted in a decision, by a dedicated group of teachers, to continue their search for answers to the difficult problems posed by the use of this teaching approach. Somehow money was made available from within other research projects to continue the work on a modest scale and a request by the Open University to make a film on teaching styles was also put to good advantage. As part of a Study Leave, one of the authors was able to work alongside two of the teachers and this, it was felt, helped us to understand the problem more clearly from each other's point of view.

A decade later group work has again become a key area of interest for primary teachers. The introduction of the National Curriculum, with its corresponding attainment targets, suggests that children will work at their own pace and that, as part of classroom organisation, groups of pupils performing at a similar level will come together to take part in joint activities. Such groups, however, will not be static but may vary according to curriculum topic and the interests of the pupils. The non-statutory guidance, *A Framework for the Primary Curriculum*, published by the National Curriculum Council, advises teachers that, 'the clarity of the National Curriculum subject requirements and detailed information about pupils' achievements will allow teachers to ensure grouping arrangements are made appropriately'. The framework, however, has nothing to say about how such groups can be helped to function effectively and the purpose of our book is to remedy this deficiency.

The book describes the efforts of teachers who worked on the various stages of the project. Where such work is referred to in the text, the names of teachers and their schools have been altered to preserve their anonymity. The emphasis is on the social rather than the cognitive aspects of group work because we came to believe that this was a crucial aspect, particularly at the stage when collaborative groups were being established. The book does not provide a set of 'tips' on how to do group work. There are too many books of this kind which in our experience have been ineffective because the contexts in which collaborative activity takes place vary considerably from school to school and from classroom to classroom within each school. What we have attempted to provide, therefore, is a set of 'guidelines' which allows teachers to devise a strategy that is suitable for their own circumstances.

The book is divided into three parts. The first part reviews the literature on collaborative group work and charts the advances made in other countries, particularly the United States of America. The second part traces the work of the SSRC ORACLE II project, *Effective Group Work in the Primary Classroom*. We seek to explain the project's failure and continue with a description of the research which took place during the following six years, ending with an account of the work of two teachers, who have been given the pseudonyms of Norma and Jean. The final part of the book looks at more practical issues including examples of the way in which teachers initiated collaborative group activity and the way in which they attempted to monitor and evaluate subsequent events. The last chapter is a more general one dealing with questions of how best to initiate changes of teaching strategy such as the use of group work in the primary classroom. Although the authors accept joint responsibility for the whole book the drafts for the first six chapters were written by Maurice Galton and the final two by John Williamson. John spent a year with the ORACLE II project and then continued the work with a team of teachers on an in-service course at his own institution in Australia.

The authors owe a debt of gratitude to a number of organisations. First, to the SSRC (now the Economic and Social Research Council) who sponsored the original research. Second, to the three local authorities who contributed sums of money to support their teachers, providing both secondments and also cover for in-service activity. Above all, however, we have individuals to thank, particularly the teachers who gave up so much of their free time to do the research and whose enthusiasm and dedication and deep concern for the welfare of their pupils encouraged us all at times when things were not going smoothly. We must thank the two researchers on the initial ORACLE II project, Roger Appleyard and Anne Yeomans, who contributed much to our early thinking. Lastly, we should like to record our appreciation of Diana Stroud's contribution. Her mastery of the IBM keyboard has meant that drafting and redrafting has caused us the minimum of pain. There are also a number of colleagues in our own and in other institutions of higher education who made significant contributions to the debate about working in groups. This helped us to formulate the ideas presented in this volume although, of course, we take full responsibility for what we have written.

1

GROUPING AND GROUP WORK

CO-OPERATION IN THE PRIMARY CLASSROOM

Let us begin by describing two contrasting incidents involving junior-aged pupils in the primary classroom. The first incident took place in a small school with a class covering a three-year age range (8+ to 10+). The teacher has been reading them the story, *Walkabout*, by James Simpson. The book recounts the adventures of some boys and girls who are the same age as the present pupils. They are flying with their father across the Australian 'outback' when the engine fails, the plane crashes and the father is killed. The children meet and are befriended by an aborigine who eventually leads them to safety.

On this particular afternoon in early spring, the teacher has finished the book and the children have been set the following task. They are to work together in groups of four to create a mime which tells the story of the plane crash and their meeting with the aborigine. I am there to observe, as part of a research project, and among the group of children that I am watching there is one very striking feature. During the lesson, one boy takes no part whatsoever in the discussion. He sits there rocking back and forward on two legs of his chair – unless the teacher is present or is looking in his direction. On these occasions he affects an air of intense concentration while listening to what the other pupils are saying. I become so interested in this pupil that I decide to abandon my plan of rotating around the groups and instead I concentrate on this boy, looking to note the points in time when he communicates with the others. However, my sheet of paper remains blank since he says nothing throughout the entire lesson. Eventually the

1

group discussion is ended and the children go out to play. After the break the groups are to rehearse their mime.

Before he goes out to play I join the boy in question and ask, with a certain diffidence,

Me I have been watching your group for some time this after-noon but I couldn't help noticing that you didn't take a very active part. You didn't appear to speak during the whole three-quarters of an hour of the lesson.

Him No. I wouldn't, would I?

Me Why is that?

Him I'm the pilot, aren't I? I'm dead and dead men don't speak, do they?

Subsequent conversation elicited the fact that he didn't like working in groups. 'It's a waste of time,' he commented and with that definitive assessment he left me and went out to play. I noticed, however, that in the playground he joined a group of peers and at once engaged in animated conversation.

Contrast this incident with another in a different school. Here the children were mostly 11 years old. In the previous year, as they later told me, they had a teacher, Mrs Wright, who was 'very keen on groups'. They liked working together because 'it was good to share ideas with your friends'. However, this year they had moved instead to Miss Vickers. She, according to the children, was 'a bit old fashioned' and 'not quite with it'. Miss Vickers made them work alone, particularly when they were writing stories. She had told them she wanted their own ideas and 'they were not to copy from each other'.

Me Did you find that difficult? I mean changing from one way of working to another.

Pupils (in a chorus) No.

Me So it doesn't matter which way you work?

Pupil No, because when we got home after school we telephoned each other and discussed our stories.

The two incidents are of interest, not only because they reflect a range of different teaching styles and attitudes on the part of the teachers but also because they demonstrate different levels of commitment from the pupils. In the first incident the boy showed a marked reluctance to engage in any kind of communication with the other pupils in his group. His reluctance, however, did not extend to playing with his peers after class. We do not know the reasons for his reluctance, whether specifically it had to do with the particular lesson or whether he disliked all kinds of drama, but his response to my questions seemed to imply that it was the teaching method itself which he disliked. The second group of pupils in Miss Vickers's class, however, showed a strong commitment to sharing ideas, so much so that they were prepared to subvert their present teacher's intention and to continue to share ideas even though they had been specifically forbidden to do so during the lesson.

There is a range of possible explanations that might be offered to account for such behaviour. According to some teachers, 'working together in a group is an adult activity and it is not to be expected that young children of primary age will find it easy. After all, children at this age are very self-centred'. Other teachers argue that the size and make-up of the group largely determine its effectiveness, while still others say that the children will work well together only if an appropriate task is chosen.

The purpose of this book is to explore some of these hypotheses. As teachers we would probably all agree that getting young children to work together is not an easy task. That being so we need some reassurance that the effort is worthwhile both in terms of the learning processes involved and also of the learning outcomes. In this book we shall look at the evidence concerning both processes and outcomes during group work and hope that readers will find it sufficiently encouraging to accept the view that such group strategies ought to be part of every teacher's repertoire.

SEATING ARRANGEMENTS IN THE PRIMARY CLASSROOM

One of the most puzzling features of today's contemporary primary school concerns this question of grouping. In most primary classrooms in the United Kingdom and overseas children sit in groups either around tables or at desks pushed together to make a square. This pattern is significantly different from that observed in many secondary schools where pupils still sit in rows with the teacher's desk centre stage at the front of the class. Like other aspects of classroom organisation the seating arrangements in the typical primary classroom say something about the prevailing

gy which governs a teacher's primary practice, that is, their
n of ideas, beliefs, fundamental commitments or values
social reality' (Apple 1979: 20). For example, the fact that
children now sit in groups of mixed sex, unlike primary
classrooms in the 1950s, indicates changes in our thinking about
gender inequality and a recognition of the way in which sex
stereotyping in the early years of schooling can exacerbate this
problem.

It is therefore surprising, when the functioning of groups in the
primary classroom is explored in greater detail, to find that practice does not appear to match the ideology which one might
suppose dictates the decision to bring pupils together in this
particular way. Sitting the children in groups would seem to
indicate a desire for children to share not only facilities but also
ideas. Yet a number of observational studies of primary classrooms has shown that verbal exchanges between pupils are
much rarer than one might have supposed (Galton *et al.* 1980;
Mortimore *et al.* 1988). Indeed in many classrooms teachers still
insist on silence during most activities. More importantly
placing children together in this way would seem to indicate a
commitment, on the part of the teacher, to a philosophy of learning based upon co-operation where children are expected to
work together towards a common end rather than competing for
individual rewards in terms of marks and stars. In stark contrast
to this view, however, is the fact that in today's primary classrooms children are assigned individual tasks and that, for the
most part, they work alone without either the intervention of the
teacher or of another pupil. In so far as a pupil does use a class-
mate as a learning resource, this is generally accomplished by
listening to the teacher talking to the other child and trying to
pick up clues from the conversation which may have relevance to
the pupil's own work (Galton 1989).

Given the fact that in many primary classrooms children,
although seated together, work alone it may be pertinent to ask
the question why those responsible for training teachers should
devote so much of their time to discussion of different forms of
organisation which are built around the seating of children in
groups. In early years, for example, the use of *curriculum tables* is
often recommended. With this organisational strategy a group of
children moves from a mathematics table to an English table and
then to an art table in rotation, as part of an integrated day. In the

4

ORACLE study (Galton *et al.* 1980) this form of rotation was often accompanied by high levels of pupil distraction and there is evidence to suggest that when the tables or desks are rearranged back in rows the level of work among pupils increases markedly (Bennett and Blundell 1983; Wheldall *et al.* 1981). Indeed, given the levels of distraction which often appear to accompany work in groups, some primary teachers have been heard to say that in their view 'children of this age are not capable of working in this way'. Presumably such teachers continue to operate a group seating arrangement because, as suggested earlier, it is a mark of the prevailing primary ideology which Colin Richards (1979) has described as liberal romanticism.

Another purpose of this book is, therefore, to explore some of the reasons why, given the emphasis there is on *seating in groups*, children *working in groups* appears to be a neglected art in the primary classroom. We propose initially, therefore, to regard group work as essentially problematic and to make no assumption that working in groups is in itself an essential element of 'good primary practice', which critics have alleged is being recommended by teacher trainers and local authority advisers to be the current prevailing orthodoxy (Alexander 1988). The first half of the book will therefore explore, in some detail, the ways in which groups are organised in the primary classroom and the ways in which children work in these groups. This discussion will be based upon evidence drawn largely from observational studies carried out in the United Kingdom. We shall then go on to consider what evidence there is to suggest that when children do actually work together in small groups there are positive outcomes, both social and cognitive, which result from this shared experience. Much of this evidence is derived from studies which have taken place outside the United Kingdom. Finally, towards the end of the first part of the book we shall attempt to derive some guidelines which might lead to effective practice in the art of group work for those who, as a result of the earlier discussions, feel that such strategies have an important part to play in the teaching and the learning of primary age children.

THE ORGANISATION OF THE PRIMARY CLASSROOM

Undoubtedly the shift towards the organisation of the primary classroom into seating groups spread rapidly during the 1960s.

While in some local authorities such as Leicestershire, Oxford and the West Riding of Yorkshire, changes in the pattern of organisation took place a decade earlier, the trend accelerated in the post-Plowden era as the abolition of selective secondary education was completed and comprehensive schools came into existence. It was during the late 1960s, when Joan Barker Lunn (1970) was carrying out her study of streaming, that the momentum grew towards the abolition of streamed classrooms in the primary school as a consequence of the abandonment of selection and the eleven plus examination in many local authorities. In Leicestershire, for example, Jones (1988) recalls in his biography of Stewart Mason, the reforming Chief Education Officer, that in the 1950s when Mason appointed Dorothea Flemming as Primary Adviser, classes still contained over fifty children, sitting 'in such tight rows that nobody could leave the room until somebody stood up'. By the beginning of the 1970s, however, most junior schools in the authority used some variation of group seating arrangements (Bealing 1972). In 1976, a survey of teachers in three local authorities, including Leicestershire, found only two out of fifty-eight classrooms where children had the traditional patterns of rows or desks. A further six either sat children in pairs but not in rows or had intricate or irregular shape patterns in which desks were lined up side by side (Galton 1981).

It would seem, therefore, that one reason for the shift towards seating in groups was possibly a reaction to the problem of mixed ability classes rather than a strategy based upon deeply held convictions about the value of co-operative learning. Before the abolition of the 11+ examination, the need to group children in this way was less obvious. For the most part teachers, like their secondary colleagues, instructed the whole class and then set pupils a series of practice examples in order to consolidate the learning (what the American researchers call seat work). With the shift to mixed ability classes, however, such a strategy was no longer possible, at least for large proportions of the time. Children in any one class might be at very different stages, even where they were all engaged on the same area of the curriculum. Thus it made sense, for some teachers, to bring together children who were working at the same stage because this made the task of instructing them easier. In their survey of primary schools, Her Majesty's Inspectors, for example, found that over 70 per cent of

6

teachers observed grouped children for mathematics in this way (DES 1978). For those who were fully committed to the child-centred approaches incorporated in Richards's 'liberal romantic' ideology this strategy posed several difficulties. Many teachers, having been convinced by the evidence which highlighted the detrimental effects, particularly for the working-class child, as a consequence of the practice of streaming, found it questionable to replace the practice of organising classes by ability with a policy of differentiation within the classroom based on exactly the same criteria. Accordingly, other criteria were proposed, for forming groups, such as interest, friendship and family. Some of these different arrangements, described by a 'Forum observer', support the view that at the time when primary schools were being rapidly 'destreamed', teachers were exploring various grouping arrangements of this kind (Forum observer, 1966).

These different purposes of grouping have different justifications and are reflected in the assumptions and suggestions put forward by various bodies offering prescriptions for effective primary practice. Thus Her Majesty's Inspectors (HMI) would appear to see the main advantage of grouping as a means of enabling teachers to provide work of an appropriate level of difficulty for pupils (DES 1978: para 8.32). The Inspectors also saw such groups as providing a more efficient way of introducing new topics or concepts to pupils since they called for more direct teaching of groups, particularly in mathematics. Groups appeared to the Inspectors to be a device, therefore, for increasing the amount of contact between teachers and pupils. In mathematics, for example, such groups 'would enable challenging questions and quick recall of number facts, including multiplication tables' which, according to the Inspectors, often require 'a lively sustained contact between teacher and a group of children' (para 5.65). The justification for this position arises from the fact that, according to the Inspectors, in suitably matched groups of this kind, able children were doing more challenging work and teachers were able to inject 'more pace into the work' and this would suggest that, for the so-called 'basic skills' in particular, groups should be set wherever pupils are able to undertake work of a similar level of difficulty.

The Plowden (1967) Committee, however, took a markedly different view. The Committee also recognised that organisation of a classroom into groups could be justified on economic grounds

in that teachers could economise on their time 'by teaching together a small group of children who are roughly at the same
stage' (para 7.54). This was not, however, a similar prescription as
HMI, which, as we have seen, recommended streaming within
the classroom, since the Plowden Committee also advised that
'the groups should be based on interest or sometimes on achievement but that they should change in accordance with the children's need' (para 8.24). Thus in the Plowden model the groups
were ephemeral and a child might find himself a member of
several different groups in the course of a week. Plowden also,
however, offered a further justification for organising a class in
this way. The committee claimed that not only did the strategy
allow more efficient use of a teacher's time, enabling increased
contact with pupils, but also it improved the quality of learning
since within these groups children 'make their meaning clear to
themselves by having to explain it to others and gain opportunities to teach as well as learn'. Group interaction was thought
to help the timid child who might be 'less shy in risking a
hypothesis in a group' (para 7.58). Apathetic children would also
benefit since they 'may be infected by the enthusiasm of a group
while other children benefit by being caught up in a thrust and
counter thrust of conversation in a small group similar to themselves' (para 7.57). In the model proposed class discussion should
be introduced towards the end when the individual pupils' contributions were complete so that 'the pieces of the jigsaw can be
fitted together . . . or seen not to fit' (para 7.60). Thus the use of
groups in the Plowden sense involved co-operative working
between children which continued even when teachers were
engaged elsewhere. The teachers' intention should be to promote
enquiry with the twin objectives of stimulating pupils' thinking
and developing their communication skills, since the teacher had
'missed the whole point if he tells the children the answers or
indicates too readily or completely how the answers may be
found' (para 6.69).

In summary, therefore, we may distinguish several purposes
of groups each giving rise to a different kind of arrangement that
needs to be clearly defined. First there is a seating arrangement
whereby children work on a similar theme or curricular area at
their own pace. We shall call such groups *seating groups* where
pupils sit in groups but do not work as a group. This is the kind
of arrangement that was favoured by Miss Vickers in the earlier

incident. Second, there is the kind of group where children work on the same task because they are at approximately the same stage of learning but they work as individuals with a minimum of co-operation. They may, for example, be working on the same mathematics or language worksheet and may check each other's answers but will be expected to work towards their own solutions. We shall call these groups *working groups*. Their main purpose is to use the teacher's time more efficiently by allowing him/ her to introduce topics, give directions and guide subsequent activity in say five groups of six children rather than for thirty individuals.

The third kind of grouping also seeks to make more effective use of the time teachers have for contact with pupils. Here, however, when the teacher is attending one group of children the other pupils are expected to continue to collaborate with each other. The task is organised in such a way that individual pupils within the group contribute to a joint outcome. Thus children may be asked to discuss how to plan a scientific experiment together making certain that the testing is fair and deciding how best to record their observations. On another occasion children might be asked to compose a mime which would then be performed in front of the rest of the class as in the first incident concerning the book, *Walkabout*. We shall call these arrangements *co-operative groups*. Usually, but not always, such *co-operative groups* will be composed of children of different ability because one purpose behind the arrangement will be to encourage slower learning pupils to learn from their more advanced peers and to encourage the latter to clarify their ideas in their role of instructor. Bennett and Dunne (1989) also make a further distinction according to the demands of the task. They distinguish situations, such as solving a mathematical problem, where children work on the same task for a single outcome, from cases where children work on individual tasks which are not identical but which must be arranged together to provide a joint outcome. This, for example, would coincide with the children's descriptions of part of Miss Vickers's lesson in the second incident where the children discussed their ideas but wrote individual stories. In one such observed lesson, for example, each child organised a number of the co-operatively derived ideas into a chapter and all the chapters were then put together to make a story book which was printed on the word processor.

9

Table 1.1 Classification of different grouping arrangements in the primary classroom

	Type	Task demand	Intended outcome	Example
1	Seating groups	Each pupil has a separate task	Different outcomes: each pupil completes a different assignment	Writing stories on themes chosen by the pupils
2	Working groups	Each pupil has the same task	Same outcome: each pupil completes the same assignment independently	Mathematics worksheet
3	Co-operative group	Each pupil has separate but related task	Joint outcome: each pupil has a different assignment	Making a map
4	Collaborative group	Each pupil has same task	Joint outcome: all pupils share same assignment	Problem solving e.g. discussing a social or moral issue

In summary, the different possible ways in which groups are organised within the typical primary classroom are shown in Table 1.1. Categories 3 and 4 in the table make a similar distinction to that used by Bennett and Dunne (1989). We shall use the term 'co-operative group work' to describe the situation where pupils work on the same task but each have individual assignments which eventually are put together to form a joint outcome. One extended example of this kind of activity involved the children in planning a day trip for the class within a limited budget. Within this objective matters such as the location, transport, food and activities had to be decided upon and planned for. Each pupil took responsibility for different aspects of the task. *Collaborative group work*, however, involves all children contributing to a single outcome and often involves problem-solving activities, particularly in cases where the group has to debate a social or moral issue and produce an agreed solution or recommendations. In practice, however, the distinction between *co-operative* and *collaborative* group work is not always as clear cut as in the above examples. In planning the outing, for example, the teacher may decide that the pupils should work in pairs. We shall, however, always refer to such cases as co-operative group work and reserve the term collaborative group work for cases where all the pupils in the group are expected to work together to produce a single outcome.

THE INCIDENCE OF GROUP WORK IN THE PRIMARY CLASSROOM

For the purposes of defining what is meant by a group we shall adopt the definition proposed by Brown (1988) that 'a group exists when two or more people define themselves as members of it and when its existence is recognised by at least one other'. Brown defines 'other' in this context as 'some person or group of people who do not so define themselves' (Brown 1988: 2–3) and for the purposes of the present discussion the other person will usually be the classroom teacher. A decade of research carried out at the University of Leicester indicates that the preferred organisational arrangement appears to be working in groups involving common tasks but individual assignments. In the original ORACLE study (Galton *et al.* 1980) much of the day's work was organised on these lines particularly in English and Mathematics. Observations of pupils showed that for nearly 80 per cent of their time in the classroom the children worked alone on individual assignments. For around 12 per cent of the remaining time they came together as a class or a register group, leaving approximately around 9 per cent of the time for co-operative or collaborative ventures. These latter activities were mainly restricted to art and craft or general studies where a practical element was involved as, for example, when the group might be working together to produce a collage for a display upon the classroom wall. At such times the teacher usually devoted her time to helping other individual pupils with work in the 'basic areas' of mathematics and language. This gave rise to a degree of asymmetry within the classroom since in contrast to the pupil working alone for 80 per cent of the time the teacher worked with different individual pupils for an equivalent proportion of the school day. Within this structure there were often high levels of distraction with pupils on a particular table tending to talk about matters other than work when the teacher's attention was

11

engaged elsewhere in the room. Even when children were encouraged to collaborate, exchanges between pupils tended to be short-lived. Less than 20 per cent of all pupil–pupil conversations extended beyond the 25 second interval before the next observation was made. Conversations between pupils tended to be of the kind which required information, such as confirming the correctness of an answer to a mathematics problem on a worksheet with the enquiry, 'What did you get for number 2?' or checking that the teacher's instructions were being followed, 'What do we do next?'. When the classroom operated in this way it is not difficult to understand why the findings of Bennett and Blundell (1983) and of Wheldall *et al.* (1981) showed that levels of distraction decreased considerably when the classroom was rearranged and the children sat individually at their desks in rows rather than in groups around tables.

Similar patterns of organisation were found in a more recent investigation of Curriculum Provision in Small Primary Schools (Galton and Patrick 1990). This study, the PRISMS project, looked at both infant and junior classrooms and found few differences across the entire age range. In this study both the base (the seating arrangement) and the team (the way in which the pupils were expected to work) organisation were recorded and compared. Table 1.2 shows the base and the team organisation. The contrasts between the two forms of organisation are very marked indeed. For example, although for 56 per cent of the time children were seated in groups they were expected to work as a group for only 5 per cent of the time during which they were observed. For 16 per cent of the time they were seated in pairs but were expected to work as a pair for only 4 per cent of the time. In contrast, although children were seated at individual desks or tables for only 7.5 per cent of the time they worked individually during 81 per cent of all observations. Even during the 20.5 per cent of the time when they were seated together as a class group (e.g. sitting on the mat listening to instructions) they were working as a class approximately only half of this period, usually because the teacher was addressing individuals within the class and either asking questions or admonishing someone for distracting behaviour. Sometimes children were made to sit alone as a punishment or to help them concentrate. This, however, was not usually very effective since 'on task' behaviour on these occasions amounted to only 63 per cent for juniors and 58 per cent for infant classes. Levels of distraction were lowest on the 10 per cent of the occasions when the children were working as a class team but on these occasions the pupils spent approximately 90 per cent of their time listening to the teacher.

Table 1.2 Base (seating) and Team (working) arrangement (% observations) in the small primary school (Galton and Patrick 1990)

Classroom organisation *(seating)*	Base %	Team %	DISTRACTION
Group	56 %	5 %	— Next lowest
Pair	16 %	4 %	
Individual	7.5 %	81 %	
Class	20.5 %	10 %	— lowest
Total	100 %	100 %	

The next lowest level of distraction occurred when the pupils were working in a group team. There was greater teacher interaction with such groups than in the ORACLE study (12.6 per cent in infant classes, 15.8 per cent in junior classes, compared to only 9.4 per cent in ORACLE classes). This was, in the main, a consequence of the fact that in most classes in small schools the age range of children is wide and pupils therefore tended to be seated and taught in groups of the same age. In these groups, when the teacher was not present, pupil–pupil talk was less than in ORACLE (13 per cent as against 19 per cent). However, unlike ORACLE, in PRISMS 55 per cent of these pupils' conversations were task related compared to just over 20 per cent in the ORACLE study. In the PRISMS analysis a wider range of curriculum activities such as games, dancing and drama were included and this may have contributed to the higher proportions of group interaction. Overall, however, the differences are not large and it would appear that the amounts of collaborative work in small schools was not much greater than that found earlier in ORACLE. Further evidence that this conclusion can be generalised to most primary schools comes from recent studies conducted in the Inner London Education Authority at infant level (Tizard *et al.* 1988) and at junior level. In the junior study, for the most part, children sat in groups but worked individually and according to the researchers 'not a great deal of collaborative work was observed' (Mortimore *et al.* 1988: 82).

These conclusions, that co-operative or collaborative group work in the primary classroom is, generally, a neglected art, suggest that the Plowden (1967) Committee, in making its recommendations, tended to underestimate the difficulties of implementation. Certainly, this would be the view of some classroom researchers, particularly in the United States. Writing in the third edition of the *Handbook of Research on Teaching*, Brophy and Good, for example, argue that,

> The small group approach requires well chosen assignments that the students are willing to engage in and able to complete successfully, as well as rules and procedures that enable students to get help (if confused) or direction (about what to do if finished) without disrupting the momentum of the teacher's lesson. Teachers . . . may find it takes too much effort to be worth the trouble.
>
> (Brophy and Good 1986: 361)

Similar views are echoed in this country by teachers taking part in a study conducted by Alexander *et al.* (1989) in which one local authority set out to change primary practice extensively in order 'to meet the educational needs of all children and, in particular, those children experiencing learning difficulties'. In many of their comments during the case studies, the teachers seemed to echo Brophy and Good's conclusions.

> Mrs. D. said that she tried to work with one group at a time but that children from other groups inevitably approached her and the reception group needed her attention at least at the beginning of every activity she set them.
>
> I don't see the point of wasting time saying the same thing to five or six different groups when I can say it once to one large group.
>
> (Alexander *et al.* 1989: 256–7)

Alexander acknowledges dilemmas facing teachers who attempt to put a policy of collaborative group work into practice where the teacher is constantly having to consider whether the drawbacks for both children and teachers outweigh the gains. Elsewhere he takes to task local authority advisers who, perhaps unwittingly, misinterpret the research findings and convey to teachers the message that 'unless pupils are interacting and collaborating within their groups there is little point in grouping them'. He argues, however, that 'there are a variety of other reasons why teachers may find it necessary to bring children together into working groups, particularly in vertically grouped classrooms or for reasons of limited resources' (Alexander 1988: 178).

THE CASE FOR WORKING COLLABORATIVELY IN GROUPS

So far we have examined the case for children working collaboratively in groups mainly in terms of the organisational advantage. Put simply, if children can be persuaded to co-operate together, independently of the teacher, it enables a greater degree of flexibility of classroom organisation so that according to one report compiled by the Education Department of Western Australia,

> Not only does the small group provide a secure and supportive base from which the students can venture out and return as they need but it also provides a manageable and flexible base from which the teacher can work to provide the best learning experience for the class.
>
> (Reid *et al.* 1982: 5)

In practice, as the research discussed so far indicates, this conclusion may be somewhat more problematic than these authors would appear to suggest. The case for persevering with collaborative group work, therefore, needs to be supported by a wider rationale than simply freeing up teacher time so that they can concentrate on the needs of individual pupils. Thus Reid *et al.* (1982) argue that there are also beneficial social, emotional and cognitive outcomes. They claim that students will

> Become actively involved in the learning process. Will be provided with a secure and supportive learning environment.
> [Students] will find that an improved teacher/student relationship can develop.

While teachers will find that 'The quality of classroom learning will improve' (Reid *et al.* 1982: IX).

15

Many of these same outcomes have been endorsed by Kerry and Sands (1982), Yeomans (1983) and Biott (1987). They argue that when pupils work together co-operatively they can learn from each other, thereby removing the stigma of failure for slow learners. Furthermore, pupils are, by this means, given a chance to work at their own pace and become less teacher dependent. Working in this way also improves individual pupil's self-image in that by working in groups the children come to respect each other's strengths and weaknesses. An additional advantage for the teacher is said to be that it enables the teacher to tailor the range of tasks which are more appropriate to the children's needs and abilities, therefore ensuring a better 'match'. Elsewhere Rowland put these arguments in a more general form

> The idea that learning takes place when individuals are put in a position of finding their own solutions fails to recognise the essential social nature of learning. Left on their own during activity with only their own resources to call upon, children may rely only upon that knowledge and those strategies with which they are familiar. Anyone trying to learn on their own easily becomes stuck into their own ways of thinking. . . . Without teachers or peers with whom to interact during the process of learning, children are liable to become entrenched in their present position. This problem arises whether the subject matter is a mathematical investigation which may require new insights, or a social enquiry which demands a new perspective on the issues of racism. The danger is that an exploratory model of learning, while intending to be a radical alternative which empowers the learner with greater autonomy, may actually have the opposite effect by protecting the learner from the challenge of social interaction. Confidence may be gained but the opportunity for growth lost.
>
> (Rowland 1987: 131)

In the following two chapters we shall review the research evidence on these points, evidence collected both here in the United Kingdom and in other countries. In Chapter 2 we shall concentrate on the research concerned with the cognitive outcomes of collaborative group work, concentrating, in particular, on the work which has been carried out in the United States, while in Chapter 3 we shall examine the social and emotional processes involved when working in collaborative groups, using the results of the ORACLE studies (Observational Research and Classroom, Learning Evaluation) which have taken place during the last decade at the University of Leicester (Galton 1987). In the remaining part of this chapter, however, we shall review the debate which has taken place among cognitive and social psychologists concerning the important determinants of pupils' thinking and learning and their relevance to co-operative ways of working.

HOW CHILDREN THINK AND LEARN

Much of contemporary primary practice, as it has developed over the years since the 1967 Plowden Report, can be traced to the growing influence of Piaget's ideas about the ways in which young children learn to think. It is beyond the scope of this chapter to engage in a detailed analysis of Piaget's views but this is done in a very concise and readable way in Wood's (1988) book, *How Children Think and Learn*. Here, we shall examine the way in which Piagetian ideas have impinged on classroom practice and, in particular, the way in which they have largely determined the use of certain forms of classroom organisation and created patterns of teacher–pupil interaction.

Wood makes the important point that Piaget was trained as a biologist so that his approach to the study of thinking and understanding of young children was essentially a scientific one. Thus in many of the classic studies the experimenter was seen to be 'outside the action' and the process largely conceived as an interaction between the object, i.e. the child, and the environment. As Wood (1988) remarks:

> Social interactions (particularly those which take place between children themselves) may facilitate the course of development by exposing a child to other points of view and to conflicting ideas which may encourage him to rethink or review his ideas. However, for Piaget, any social facilitation of development only works when the child's understanding, based on his commerce with nature is in an appropriate state of readiness for change.
>
> (Wood 1988: 16)

The idea that there are stages of development and that children cannot be taught to operate at higher stages until they have

17

mastered all the previous ones has important implications for teaching and curriculum planning. If we accept the now commonly held view, endorsed in the National Curriculum, that children are entitled to a curriculum covering all the major areas of human experience, then there has to be a theory of development that enables teachers to select appropriate experiences which will promote effective learning. Piaget's theories offer an important way of achieving this match. However, too rigid acceptance of this 'stage theory' can, in certain particular ways, 'de-skill' the teacher. Although Piaget himself had very little to say about the implications of his ideas for teaching, those who have interpreted his theories have usually placed the emphasis on the role of *teacher as facilitator* rather than *teacher as instructor*. The metaphors used to represent this process are typically horticultural. The teacher, like the gardener, with watering can in one hand, a bag of fertiliser in the other, moves among the plants providing moisture and nutriment. The gardener's skill lies in maintaining exactly the right conditions to support maximum growth and this will vary according to the plant's particular needs. In the analogy the teacher's plants are the pupils, the fertiliser the resources and the combination of soil and water the appropriate environment to motivate the child into reconstructing her existing view of the world.

This metaphor is an extremely powerful one and is reflected in the narrative accounts of teachers (Cortazzi 1990). When asked to describe an event in the classroom which gave them most satisfaction the vast majority of teachers in the sample narrated an event whereby a particular pupil, just like the plant, made a significant spurt in growth. None of these teachers attributed this success to their instruction but rather to the choice of the topic and its capacity to arouse the pupil's interest and therefore increase motivation. Thus, besides the difficulties of organising working in groups, already discussed, there appears to be a strong internalised theory reinforcing the teacher's perception that since children largely learn by constructing their own view of the world and not through being told things by the teacher they are equally unlikely to be able to learn from each other when in many circumstances what they are told by one pupil may be wrong. It is significant, for example, that even Rowland, who was quoted earlier, supports group activity largely on social rather than cognitive grounds. Indeed in the same account he describes a lesson where he intervenes to instruct a pupil about fractions but he emphasises that this comes about only because the pupil was ready for this re-construction having reached a stage in his problem solving where he needed to express the data as fractions of the whole (Rowland 1987).

It follows from this that to justify the effort involved in setting up and maintaining collaborative group work it is necessary to look beyond Piaget for alternative views of the learning process. One such viewpoint is provided by the Soviet psychologist, Vygotsky. Recently there has been a revival of interest in his work (Day 1983; Wood 1988). Unlike Piaget, Vygotsky argues that all higher mental functions are developed through interaction either with adults or more capable peers. During these interactions the more capable people 'serve as mediators'. They focus attention on relevant dimensions of the environment, supply strategies for 'dealing with problems' (Day 1983: 157). According to Vygotsky, the skills which the child learns in this way are internalised through a prolonged developmental process and once internalised the skills learnt are no longer subject to the same rules that controlled them previously during the interaction with adults and peers. Without the interaction with others children cannot internalise new skills and only after a skill has been internalised can it be carried out independently. There is, therefore, a gap between what children can do in conjunction with other people and what they can do alone.

Vygotsky, therefore, stresses the co-operative nature of learning:

> Learning awakens a variety of developmental processes that are able to operate only when the child is interacting with people in his environment and in co-operation with peers. Once these processes are internalised they become part of the child's developmental achievement.
>
> (Vygotsky 1978: 90)

Wood (1988: 25) argues that this concept 'leads to a very different view of readiness for learning from that offered by Piagetian theory', since 'readiness' in Vygotskian terms depends not only upon the state of the child's existing knowledge but also upon his *capacity to learn with help*. In developing these ideas Vygotsky makes use of a key concept which he calls 'zone of proximal development'. This is defined as the difference between what children can do independently and what they can accomplish with the support of another individual who is more knowledgeable and skilled. One of the problems with this concept, however, is that it is more difficult to define operationally than are Piaget's stages because the extent of the zone clearly depends, among other things, on the quality of instruction received. The theory, however, does give validity to the claim by those who argue that the quality of classroom learning improves with the effective use of co-operative groups and that the composition of such groups should contain pupils at different stages of intellectual development.

SOCIAL AND EMOTIONAL EFFECTS OF WORKING IN GROUPS

Two decades of classroom research has led to increasing emphasis being placed upon learning as a social as well as a cognitive activity. In particular, it is well recognised (Burns 1982; Wells and Maxwell 1976) that the way individuals perceive themselves is a major determinant of their subsequent behaviour governing both relationships with other people and the motivation which the person brings to a particular task. Working in groups clearly has an important effect on what Brown (1988) calls a person's 'social identity' which is one of the components of a person's self-concept, the other being their own personal evaluation (Turner 1982). Thus a person's self-concept will be formed partly by the way in which he or she evaluates the interactions with their peers and partly through their identification with certain characteristics of the particular group to which they may belong, as for example when pupils say that they are 'on the top table for mathematics'. Earlier research tended to concentrate on the dynamics of being an individual within a group, particularly in relation to the roles taken by different members but more recently increasing attention has been paid to the group characteristics which give rise to a sense of social identity and govern relationships to other groups.

One pioneering study was carried out by Deutsch (1949) who conducted a number of experiments on students attending a psychology course. The students were randomly assigned to two different types of groups. In one group students were told that they would all receive the same grade and that this would be determined by comparing the group's performance, as a whole, with other groups in the class. The other group of students were told they would receive individual grades according to how well they performed in their group. Deutsch found that the groups who were dependent on each other for their final grade were more co-operative with one another, expressed more liking for one another, showed less signs of aggression and in general were rated more productive. More controlled studies (Rosenbaum *et al.* 1980) where the groups were randomly assigned to different experimental and control groups confirmed Deutsch's earlier finding. Thus co-operative rather than competitive working appears to have positive consequences for judgements we make about our own worth.

Clearly such changes develop over time. Most of us would acknowledge that we experience some anxiety when we are placed with a group of people initially, even in cases where the people are known to us. At first there will be tension between the desire to protect our own personal identity and the need to help contribute to the social identity which can be expected to develop as the work of the group progresses. In the extreme case, the boy who was observed as part of the group developing a mime about the book *Walkabout*, described in the opening incident in this chapter, sought to preserve his personal identity at the expense of social identity by disengaging from the group altogether. In the second incident, presumably, the children's personal identity had become closely bound up with the social identity of the group so that a strong commitment to co-operation existed even when an authority figure, Miss Vickers, tried to prevent this collaboration. Hence the process of becoming an effective collaborative group of pupils is a dynamic one during which, as Moreland and Levine (1982) point out, not only do individual members adjust according to the demands of the group but also the group itself adjusts in order to accommodate the needs of its individual members. Unsuccessful groups are likely to be those where these kinds of dynamic changes do not proceed smoothly. We need to consider, therefore, how teachers can manage this process effectively.

The above discussion would suggest that being part of a group will involve its members in taking on different roles from time to time. Typically, however, most of the discussion of roles tends to take place around the rather crude distinction of leaders and followers. Yet studies of groups point to a very complex system of role differentiation. Bales (1950; 1953), for example, distinguishes between instrumental and expressive activities and suggests that different members of the group act out different roles in helping the group function effectively. Instrumental activity is that which helps the group successfully to complete its task as in our example of producing a mime. During this process certain tensions arise because there may be disagreements about the best way to proceed and these tensions need to be reduced by means of expressive activities. Often, for example, a member of the group may make a funny remark giving rise to laughter and so reducing possible tension. Bales suggests that the same person may often find it difficult to provide both task and social emotional leadership within the group.

Brown (1988) in reviewing studies on the role of leadership in groups points to an important dilemma among those who are trying to improve the effectiveness of collaborative group work. The ability of one person to satisfy the instrumental and expressive leadership roles within a group would clearly be dependent on factors such as the individual's personality. In many situations where the leadership role is associated with formal status, such as the headteacher of a school or the managing director of a business, there is no alternative but to subject such individuals to training in order to improve their skills and repair their deficiencies even though with some personality types it may be very difficult to modify their typical behaviour. In the classroom situation, however, it may be preferable for the teacher not to seek to modify the behaviour of certain pupils so that they become more effective leaders but rather to manipulate the situation, particularly the composition of the groups, so that appropriate persons are found to match the demands of the particular task (Fiedler *et al.*, 1976). Brown summarises these findings as follows,

Those in high status positions are often referred to as leaders and it is often believed that certain individuals possess traits which equip them for this role. Most evidence suggests otherwise. Leaders are those who have attributes which can help the group achieve particular task goals, or are those whose personalities are well matched to particular situations. Where the match is poor the group is often less effective. Improving the fit between a leader and the situation is the objective of leadership training programmes, although controversy exists over whether to change the leader, the situation or both.

(Brown 1988: 88)

If we accept this conclusion then it follows that the definition for effective group work in the classroom concerns not only the capacity of the groups to complete tasks successfully but also the capacity for each pupil to be able to take on different roles within the group according to the nature of the task and the composition of the other members. In evaluating a pupil's capacity to work well in groups a teacher therefore needs to be able to categorise pupils and to encourage them to analyse for themselves their own performance in order to regulate their own self-improvement.

We shall examine the practical implications of this statement in the central chapters of the book. First, however, we shall review the empirical evidence relating to group work in the classroom including questions about its effectiveness. In the next chapter we shall look at the research connected with the instrumental functioning of groups while in the third chapter we shall consider issues related to expressive functioning. This latter work will describe in detail the second phase of the ORACLE project, *Effective Group Work in the Primary Classroom*, which took place during the early 1980s and which was then extended during other successive projects in order to clarify some of the issues which arose during the first phase of the inquiry.

2

GROUP WORK AND TASK COMPLETION

The research evidence

RESEARCH INTO GROUP WORK

In this chapter we shall look at the evidence that supports the adage, 'a problem shared is a problem solved'. The source of this evidence comes mainly from studies carried out in the United States of America but contributions from researchers in the United Kingdom, Holland and Israel will also be considered. In examining this evidence an important distinction needs to be kept in mind. The work from the United States has, for the most part, concerned itself with answering this question by comparing the outcomes achieved when pupils worked in groups and when they did not. In the United Kingdom, however, more attention has been given to the process by which a successful outcome was achieved. In this way, therefore, the studies may be seen as complementary.

We shall begin first with the American research. In the previous chapter mention was made of the early work of Deutsch (1949). Deutsch compared groups which were 'negatively independent', that is where success by one person in the group meant that others had to recognise failure, against groups with 'positive interdependence' where the actions of one member of the group benefited everyone else. We usual define these conditions as a difference between 'co-operation' and 'competition'.

THE JIG-SAW CLASSROOM

One strand of American research has, through a series of experimental studies, investigated not only questions of co-operation versus competition, but also the effects of co-operative groups when competing with each other. It is argued that if every member of a group has to make a contribution towards the group's outcome, when the group is in competition with other groups within the classroom, this will not only create a greater sense of solidarity but also ensure 'peer-tutoring'. Peer tutoring (Goodlad and Hirst 1989) is where the more capable members of the group help those who have difficulties in mastering the task. Such an arrangement lends itself admirably to the development of what, in Chapter 1, was defined as *co-operative* grouping, where each individual, within the group, has a separate but related task to complete when working towards a joint outcome. Some of the most influential ideas concerning this kind of arrangement have been developed by Aronson *et al.* (1978) with the construction of what they termed, the *jig-saw classroom*. In this arrangement the class is divided up into groups and then sub-divided into pairs and each pair is given a specific task connected with the overall project.

Let us, for example, consider the task of planning a day's outing in which four areas of decision making must be covered. These are (a) the selection of a suitable location, (b) the provision of food for a picnic, (c) the choice of transport and (d) the choice of activities to take place during the day. The teacher sets the maximum cost per person and the groups have to draw up a plan within this figure. Clearly the activities are interdependent since the choice of location will influence how the class travels and the cost of transport will determine how much money is left over for food. Each group has to present its overall plan to the class and one of these will be selected and acted upon (the winners).

Figure 2.1 shows the initial classroom layout (Stage 1). Each pair of children is denoted by a number and a letter. The pair (1T) work on Table 1 and are concerned with transport whereas pair 4L are working on Table 4 and are concerned with the question of a suitable location. Each pair works together, in relative isolation, discussing and exchanging ideas. At a suitable point, the children then move tables and become letter groups as shown in Stage 2 of Figure 2.1. The timing of this change may arise either because the teacher has decided, arbitrarily, that the pairs of children are not likely to get much further in isolation or because a specific period has been allowed for Stage 1 of the proceedings. At Stage 2 the pairs of children from the number tables who were discussing transport now come together (Table T) and pool ideas. The same

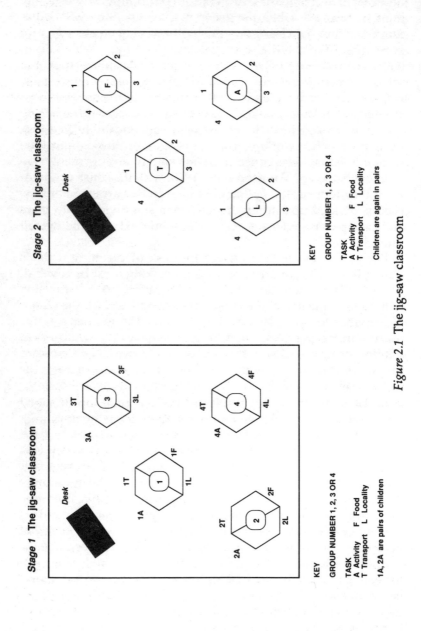

Stage 1 The jig-saw classroom

Desk

KEY

GROUP NUMBER 1, 2, 3 OR 4

TASK
A Activity   F Food
T Transport   L Locality

1A, 2A are pairs of children

Stage 2 The jig-saw classroom

Desk

KEY

GROUP NUMBER 1, 2, 3 OR 4

TASK
A Activity   F Food
T Transport   L Locality

Children are again in pairs

Figure 2.1 The jig-saw classroom

happens on the remaining tables which are devoted to food (F), location (L) and activities (A) respectively. Again, at a suitable point in time the children move back to their number tables (Stage 1). Now, however, they should have many more ideas to share in deciding their overall plan.

The procedure described above is more sophisticated than the one used by Aronson *et al.* (1978). In their studies, all pupils had to learn the other pairs' sub-tasks so that any member of a number group was capable of making a presentation on behalf of another pair. Aronson *et al.* (1978) argued that the possibility of being selected by the teacher to present other people's material increased the motivation to co-operate. Other studies using the same or similar approaches have claimed that this kind of grouping also leads to improved attitudes (Blaney *et al.* 1977) and also increases self-esteem among the group members. It is also said to improve academic achievement, particularly of children from ethnic backgrounds (Lucker *et al.* 1976; Slavin 1986).

COMPETITION VERSUS CO-OPERATION

By far the most ambitious series of studies has, however, been carried out by Robert Slavin and his colleagues. Unlike the above example of planning a class outing, where the successful group was the one whose plan was chosen by the teacher, Slavin argues that success must be more clearly defined by some form of extrinsic reward. Slavin's analogy is that of a team involved in competitive sport. Within a class teams are made up of high, average and low performing students with a mix of boys and girls and, where appropriate, with pupils of different racial or ethnic backgrounds. Each team is, as far as possible, representative of the whole class structure. Each member of the team has to accept responsibility for the learning of all individuals within a team and not just their own progress. Usually, while the pupils are able to help each other during team practices, they have to perform on their own when taking the test on which the group score is based. Individual scores of team members are then combined to form the overall team score. This procedure, developed by De Vries and Slavin (1978), is known as the teams-games-tournament approach (TGT). The procedure has been modified into a student-teams-achievement division (STAD) by Slavin (1978) where quizzes are used and each individual's contribution to the team's score is weighted to allow for capability, based upon previous performance. Thus a pupil with only two spellings correct on a previous test and who, on the next occasion, gets six right makes a bigger contribution to the team score than another pupil who having scored six last time only improves her result to eight.

In an analysis of some thirty-three studies in both elementary and secondary classrooms, Slavin (1983a) has claimed that twenty-two showed a significant positive effect on student achievement, particularly when the study involved student team learning techniques. It is also claimed that these arrangements have improved inter-group relations and, as we have already seen, this is said to be particularly true of groups with students from different ethnic backgrounds. When the teams games approach was combined with a jig-saw arrangement the result was a considerable improvement of self-esteem of all the group members.

There are, however, a number of problems in interpreting these results, which are discussed in a review of this work by Bennett (1985). Bennett argues that a major problem of this body of research has been 'comparability of treatment in experimental and control groups' (Bennett 1985: 109). To begin with the tasks which were given to the experimental group, the ones used, for example, in the TGT approach, were usually highly structured while the control group were given more general tasks. Teachers in the control sample were advised simply to use 'a more traditional approach'. The differences in outcome between the experimental group and the control group could therefore have been a function of the nature of the curriculum task, the use of grouping and non-grouping strategies or the influence of the teacher. More importantly, none of the studies actually observed the experimental group while they were engaged in 'group' activity. Therefore, even if the validity of the results is accepted there is little information on offer to the teacher about how positive effects of the process can be maximised. This is particularly true of much of the American research because it was not conducted under normal classroom conditions and there is considerable evidence that, in the study of teaching, the results of artificially contrived experiments do not always match the results obtained during a normal classroom lesson (Dunkin and Biddle 1974). Nevertheless Bennett (1985: 112) concludes, 'if the goal is individual achievement, it would seem that some kind of group incentive system is required together with a demand for individual accountability'.

A different approach has been used by Johnson and Johnson (1976) and Johnson *et al.* (1976; 1978; 1979). Their suggested arrangement is much closer to the collaborative group strategy as defined in Chapter 1. Unlike Slavin's approach, where the individuals complete the assignment by themselves and the scores of individuals are then aggregated, the Johnsons recommend that the outcome of the group's activity should consist of a single assignment sheet. For example, the group could be asked to complete a mathematical crossword together. In addition, the groups are judged, not only on how well they do on the group task, but also on how well they have worked together in carrying out the assignment. In an analysis of large numbers of studies, Johnson *et al.* (1981), claim that this collaborative structure promotes higher achievement at all age levels and in all subject areas on tasks demanding a range of skills such as concept attainment, predicting and evaluating. In all they reviewed one hundred and nine studies which compared co-operative and competitive structures and found that sixty-five showed the superiority of the co-operative method and only eight went against this trend with the remaining thirty-six demonstrating no significant differences between the experimental and control groups.

Slavin (1983b), however, rejects this assessment. He conducted a similar analysis to the Johnsons but eliminated all studies which lasted two weeks or less. This ruled out all the Johnson *et al.*'s own studies and led Slavin to the opposite conclusion that individual rewards are a necessary feature of effective co-operation among pupils in groups. Other researchers have also been critical of the relatively short length of time during which many of the experiments cited by the Johnsons were conducted (Cotton and Cook 1982; McGlynn 1982). These writers also object to the fact that the majority of the 109 studies in Johnson *et al.*'s (1981) analysis were not carried out in classrooms. For these reasons American researchers tend to support Slavin's conclusions rather than those of the Johnsons.

There is, however, another possible explanation of these contradictory results not discussed by these American critics. Mention was made in the opening chapter of Moreland and Levine's (1982) hypothesis that different socialisation processes

29

operated at different stages during the group process. It has also been shown that even after very difficult initial encounters within a group, strong solidarity between members will still often develop, arising partly because, as Aronson and Mills (1959) argue, the individual members of the group have to justify having to submit to the unpleasant initial experience by reasoning, 'If I endured all that anxiety it must have been worth it in the end'. It may, therefore, be that Johnson *et al.*'s (1981) conclusions relate to the initiation period while those of Slavin relate to a different stage when a group's 'social identity' has been established. Such a hypothesis, if true, has important consequences for teaching since it would suggest that a teacher needs to employ a different kind of pedagogy at different stages of a group's activity. These implications will be discussed in much greater detail in Chapter 4.

Before leaving the American research, mention must also be made of the work of Noreen Webb, who, unlike both Slavin and the Johnsons, has studied, albeit in very general terms, the verbal interaction which takes place between pupils in groups. Webb (1983) is chiefly concerned to explore the characteristics of pupils within a group who offer help and those who receive the help. She makes a distinction between two different kinds of help. The first kind of help, *explanations*, consists of 'step by step descriptions of how to solve a problem or detailed accounts of how to correct an error' (Webb 1985: 33). *Terminal* help, the second kind of aid, consists 'of brief responses to other students' questions' as for example, when a pupil gives another 'the correct answer to a problem without describing how to obtain it' or when the pupil detects or corrects another student's error 'without explaining how to obtain the correct answer' (Webb 1985: 33). Of these two kinds of help Webb (1983) suggests that her results support the conclusion that explanations have a positive effect on pupil achievement whereas terminal help or ignoring requests for help has a negative effect. This accounts for her earlier finding that typically, the degree of interaction within a group is not a major determinant of pupil achievement, since the effects of the two different kinds of help tend to cancel each other out.

In later studies Webb (1985; 1989) has explored the detailed characteristics of groups. She found, for example, that girls were more likely than boys to ask general questions such as, 'Is that right?' Or 'I have done number 2. What do we do next?' Webb (1985) also investigated the behaviour of pupils of different ability.

A pupil's ability was defined relative either to the scores of the other pupils in the class (absolute ability) or of the other pupils in the group (relative ability). Both the absolute and the relative ability position of a pupil within a group predicted their interaction within the group. Able students tended to give the most explanations while pupils of low ability (both absolute and relative) tended to be more willing to receive explanations. Webb explains this finding in terms of the pupils' perceptions of their own worth. The more able students tended to believe that their capacity for learning depended largely on their own efforts whereas slower learning pupils tended to attribute their performance to the influence of others such as their teachers.

Webb's findings tend to be consistent with the hypothesis advanced earlier that initial behaviour in groups changes over time so that a group composition that works best in the short term may not still be the best one for achieving longer term objectives. The situation is, however, quite complicated. Although the frequency of explanations seems to increase in mixed ability groups these exchanges tend to take place between the pupils of relative high and relative low ability. Pupils of relative medium ability are largely left out of the interaction. Webb (1985) also stresses the need for teachers to structure the task in order to promote verbal communication. According to Webb (1985: 37) 'such instructions must be embedded within the class norms that encourage cooperation'. Finally, if rewards are offered then these should not be solely for the group product but should also take into account the extent to which all pupils in the group have contributed to the learning. Without this additional requirement in the extreme case, the most able pupil in the group will do most of the work in producing the product.

OTHER RELEVANT STUDIES

A number of other studies appears to sit between the American research, with its emphasis on competitive and non-competitive structures and their effect on outcomes, and recent British studies, which have tended to concentrate on identifying various types of interactions taking place within groups and the various factors which either support or inhibit these exchanges. In Israel, for example, there have been a number of studies which have investigated the use of co-operative group learning methods in teaching science at junior and high school level (Sharan 1980; Sharan *et al.* 1984).

Hertz-Lazarowitz and Karsenty's (1990) experimental study, for example, was carried out using nineteen experimental classes and ten control classes. The experimental group attended workshops where they were given advice on how to guide small group instruction as well as participating in activities designed to help them construct small groups and organise the learning. For the study itself a jig-saw arrangement, with peer tutoring, was used in the experimental groups to teach a topic on photosynthesis. The control group presented the same material but in a traditional classroom-laboratory setting in which the tutor presented the material to the students by means of lectures and demonstrations. Pupils were pre-tested on their knowledge of biology and then tested again at the end of the experiment on the topic of photosynthesis as well as on a more general test of science processes. In addition the students completed a learning environment inventory (Wallberg and Anderson 1968), subsequently modified by Fraser (1986) for use in science lessons. A questionnaire designed to measure the pupil's self-esteem based on an earlier instrument developed by Aronson *et al.* (1978) was also used.

On the various test measures the experimental group either obtained superior or equivalent scores to the controls. Furthermore the students' self-esteem in the co-operative groups was higher and they expressed more satisfaction with their learning environment than did the pupils who were taught in the traditional manner. Although differences in self-esteem were small, this finding could partly be attributed to the fact that the experiment was conducted over five teaching sessions with a very short time for pupils' self-image to undergo significant change.

Hertz-Lazarowitz (1990) has also argued that as pupils move from working on tasks individually to working in groups their behaviour changes over time. In the process they need to acquire and use two 'extra learning skills' which she terms 'transitional skills' and 'group maintenance skills'. Transitional skills help the pupil shift from solitary to interactive behaviour and group maintenance skills help the group, as a whole, to keep on-task. Only when both sets of skills are acquired can a group engage in complex cognitive interactions of the kind that are involved in group investigations and problem solving (Hertz-Lazarowitz

1990: 28). Becoming an effective member of a group is therefore a two-stage process. Teachers need to use different strategies to foster collaboration according to the stage the pupils have reached. These strategies should focus on aspects of organisation, task content and methods of communication (Hertz-Lazarowitz 1990: 29).

Another experimental study in which both academic achievement and self-esteem have been used as outcome variables was carried out by Roeders (1989) in Dutch elementary schools. Teachers in the experimental group were drawn from three schools and involved children in the 4th and 6th grades. These teachers and pupils were compared with an equivalent sample from three other control schools. The experimental group were given a special handbook setting out different methods of engaging pupils in co-operative group work, including the jig-saw and peering tutoring method as used by Hertz-Lazorowitz and Karsenty (1990). In all the in-service course lasted fifteen weeks and the teachers were also encouraged to exchange experiences at other times with video tapes used to demonstrate different techniques. Significant effects were present with respect to reading comprehension and arithmetic achievement scores, with experimental groups showing greater gains in learning than the control groups. The experimental group also showed slightly more improvement in motivation and in self-esteem.

Teachers were also asked to evaluate the different kinds of group work on a five-point scale. Group discussion where the group contributed to a common outcome was judged to be the most useful method (rated 4.00) and Slavin's student team tournament method the lowest (2.40 rating). Group investigations, where pupils worked on individual tasks, within a common theme was judged to be the most difficult to implement (rating 2.75) with tandem (peer tutoring) the easiest (rating 4.00). The jig-saw method was judged to be the most time consuming (2.75) with peer tutoring (1.00) and group discussion (1.50) the simplest. Pupils had the most negative reaction to Slavin's student team approach (2.80) and the highest positive affect to peer tutoring (3.80). Overall, group discussion followed by group investigation was thought to be the most attractive method, with peer tutoring next followed by the jig-saw classroom. However, Roeder's samples were very small and the experiment conducted over a relatively short period of single term. Neither of the experiments discussed in this section observed the interaction of pupils, while engaged in the experiment. It cannot clearly be demonstrated, as a result of these studies, that the effects were totally due to children co-operating with each other. What is of most value about Roeder's (1989) study is that it was conducted under normal classroom conditions and not, as in some American experiments, with small groups in isolation from the rest of the class. It is also interesting that the European teachers should strongly reject all kinds of group activity which had a competitive element built into the process.

BRITISH RESEARCH

In this section we shall examine research which has taken place into grouping in the United Kingdom since the 1970s. An account of the work which has taken place at the University of Leicester forming part of the ORACLE project and of succeeding research studies will, however, be left until the next chapter.

Much of the earlier British research is reviewed by Yeomans (1983). Her review begins with the work of Abercrombie (1960; 1970) who investigated why medical students who were able to solve problems, when presented in a familiar format, were unable to do so when the same problems were presented in a slightly different way. Abercrombie found that group discussion helped these students solve such problems and, in particular, improved the ability of the students to discriminate between facts and opinions, to resist false conclusions and to bring fresh strategies to their attempts to solve new problems without being adversely influenced by past failure. At school level, however, much of the earlier research has concerned language acquisition. As part of the Schools Council Project into *Effective Use of Reading*, Lunzer and Gardner (1979) encouraged pupils to explore collaboratively the meaning of text in a given reading task. The curriculum material was deliberately chosen to be interesting and enjoyable and it was not, therefore, possible in this study, to estimate the relative contributions made to the success of the programme by the curriculum material and by the group collaboration.

Other small-scale studies (Barnes *et al.* 1969; Barnes and Todd 1977) have explored the value of small groups for encouraging exploratory talk. Barnes and Todd (1977) for example made a number of small-scale studies involving children in the lower secondary school. These pupils worked in unsupervised small groups on tasks set by the teacher. The teachers were often surprised by the quality of the discussion and cited a number of instances where the contribution of a pupil within the group far outweighed the quality of their performance during class discussion. Barnes and Todd recorded a number of examples of such talk and argued that children are able to increase their understanding in such situations without needing to call on an adult resource. Similar conclusions were advanced by Tough (1977) as part of another Schools' Council Project, *Communication Skills in Early Childhood*. Tough studied language development in nursery and infant children and concluded that even at the earliest age such children were capable of engaging in the extended exploratory discussions.

None of these studies, however, looked in any detail at the relationship between the groups' interaction and pupil achievement. There was a 'taken for granted' assumption, implicit in all these studies that because the children were talking they were therefore learning. One of the earliest attempts to explore the context in which such discussions took place and to examine their effect on performance was carried out as part of the initial ORACLE project by Tann (1981). Tann examined the interaction processes taking place during group work in some detail and then related these effects to different grouping policies. In her study children were given four tasks and the discussions were recorded and analysed. For this task Tann used a radio-microphone with a multi-track tape-recorder, a technique later also used by Bennett *et al.* (1984). Each child's conversation was recorded separately and then combined to provide the 'total' discussion for analysis. The tasks chosen all involved 'creative English', demanding both reasoning and imaginative skills. Ninety-six separate 20 minute discussions were analysed. Since most of the tasks set were open-ended (i.e. there was no one single correct answer) the criteria for success varied from group to group. To achieve success the group had to solve the problem as they defined it and in a manner which was acceptable to the entire group. Tann identified three key stages in the discussion process. The first, labelled *orientation*, involved pupils in such tasks as defining problems, interpreting the task and setting limits on the activity. The second stage, *development*, involved what we now call 'brain-storming' in which the pupils generated ideas and evolved reasoning strategies. The third *concluding* stage was marked by increasing acceptance of each other's ideas and more progressive focusing on specific strategies necessary for a successful resolution of the problem.

Tann found that the three main determinants of success involved the pupils' ability to raise questions, to listen attentively to each other and to manage disputes whenever these arose. These kinds of interactions can all be subsumed under Webb's (1985) category of explanatory help. However, in general, the analysis of the tape-recordings revealed that there was very little use of questioning by either the teachers or the pupils. Pupils were given very little instruction about 'how to work in groups'. Tann also replicated Webb's (1983) findings that boys tended to offer more suggestions whereas, in contrast, girls tended to be more consensus orientated and avoided challenging each other. Unlike Webb's (1985) study, however, there were 'interaction' effects in that low ability male members of mixed ability groups tended to take an active part in discussion whereas slow learning girls within these groups tended to remain very silent and allowed the most able girl to emerge as leader.

. Like many other studies of grouping, Tann's observations were carried out in highly structured directed situations and it is not therefore possible to generalise from them to normal classroom practice. Another difficulty in seeking to interpret her results concerns the way in which Tann identified success. By establishing the group's satisfaction with their efforts as one criterion of success, together with satisfactory completion of the task, Tann makes it difficult to evaluate how far each factor was directly related to the quality of the discussion. Nevertheless Tann's research is noteworthy because it is the first attempt, in the United Kingdom, to study the processes of group interaction in a systematic way and its findings generally support the work of Webb and other researchers in the United States.

Tann's work also points to the complex nature of group activity in suggesting that different teaching strategies may be required for different topics, for different group compositions, and for different stages of a task. The research of Biott reported in Biott (1987) supports this view. In Biott's study the early stages of group discussion were observed to be mainly concerned with precision matters. There was little evidence that children listened to each other's views. Over time, however, there was some evidence that the nature of tasks was being reconsidered and that ideas for accomplishing them were reviewed. Biott argues that many teachers, observing the lack of any real achievement in the early stages of the activity, abandon group work. This, in turn, causes pupils to develop low expectations about the effectiveness of working together, since the teacher always ends the activity before anything worthwhile has been accomplished. Biott also argues that the notion of leadership within groups is a questionable one since

> the official leader did little more than give turns, do the writing or read out the task and children who were expected to be leaders were sometimes bossy and impatient. They acted in ways which precluded slow pace reflection, tentative thinking aloud, question raising and exploratory testing of ideas.
>
> (Biott 1987: 10)

Biott suggests, therefore, that it is more useful to identify the roles of group members in terms of the responsibility they take for maintaining or raising the quality of the groups' efforts. Among such roles were:

> Encouraging and supporting others especially weaker members.
> Holding the group together in difficult moments.
> Questioning others to invite participation.
> Expressing doubt in a way which invites others to comment.
> Trying to express a half formulated idea in a way which encourages others to join.
> Summarising progress in a tentative way and slowing the pace to make the group more reflective or speeding it up to test more ideas.
>
> (Biott 1987: 11)

Like Webb (1989) Biott argues strongly for the need to develop a structured approach to group work, particularly shared understanding between the teacher and the pupils of the rules regarding group activity. He also points to the need to help pupils recognise the quality of their own participation within a group by letting pupils know, not only how valuable a particular contribution to group discussion might have been (in general terms), but also by providing specific examples which explain just why this was so. Such advice is, however, not easy to put into practice and we shall repeatedly return to these issues throughout the book.

More recently a number of studies, designed to explore some of the questions raised by the American research described earlier, have been carried out by Neville Bennett and his associates (Bennett 1985). In his earlier studies six classrooms of infant-aged children were selected and the conversations recorded by attaching live and imitation radio-microphones on every child in the class. In this way neither the pupils nor the teacher knew which groups were actually being recorded. Transcripts of both mathematics and language tasks were collected and unlike other studies in junior classrooms two-thirds of pupil–pupil talk was found to be task related. However, only a small proportion of all this talk was what Bennett termed 'task enhancing' – helping to improve the pupils' performance on the task. Most of the conversations recorded concerned the amount of work each pupil had done or involved arguments relating to the use of materials. The most frequent kinds of task enhancement conversation concerned what Webb (1985) labelled 'explanations' but only 8 per cent of all talk recorded could be included under this category. Even so most of these requests for help were of a low order, for example, Bennett quotes one pupil asking 'how many twos in fifty-four?'. As in the American studies described earlier, Bennett also found variations according to the composition of the groups. Instructional input was highest in groups consisting of high and average ability pupils compared to groups made up of low and average ability pupils. In the groups containing above-average pupils the mean proportion of instructional input was 15 per cent compared to 2 per cent in the low ability groups.

Because the sample was only a very small one (six classrooms) further studies were carried out on the effect of group composition (Bennett and Cass 1989). Using the judgements of teachers to determine the attainment level of pupils within their class, nine groups of 11 and 12 year old children were studied while engaged on a computer assisted learning task involving historical sites and settlement patterns. Pupils had to make a number of decisions regarding the most suitable field for a settlement which they deduced by using a number of general principles which they inferred from the data provided. Comparisons were made between homogeneous groups consisting of either high, average, or low attainers each with two boys and one girl and a variety of heterogeneous or mixed groupings. The same technique of radio-microphone recording was used as in earlier studies and the same categories, reported in Bennett (1985), distinguishing between instructional and procedural management talk, were used. The highest number of interactions was found in the mixed group and the lowest in the homogeneous group (805.8 to 277.6). Within the mixed groups the greatest number of interactions was found in the group containing two low and one high attainer. Contrary to other studies Bennett and Cass (1989) found that girls tended to speak more frequently, despite the fact that there were fewer of them in each group. When talk was broken down into sub-categories then mixed groups still had more interaction in all cases.

In examining the quality of these discussions Bennett and Cass (1989) made a distinction between the explanations offered and the appropriateness of the premise on which the explanation was based. While 43 per cent of explanations were both correct and appropriate, 42 per cent were correct but inappropriate: in each case most of these explanations were offered by the high attainers in the group. A little under a third of all instructional talk consisted of suggestions. Of these 54 per cent were from the higher attainers compared to 32 per cent from low attainers and fourteen per cent from average attainers; 69 per cent of all these suggestions were inappropriate yet a large number of them were accepted by other members of the group. The tendency to accept inappropriate suggestions was twice as great in mixed groups than in homogeneous groups.

Immediately after the task was completed each child was given a post-task interview. Three-quarters of the children were able to recall the decision regarding the site with a clear sex difference in favour of girls 90 per cent of whom recalled correctly compared to 71 per cent of the boys. When asked the reasons why a particular site was chosen, mixed groups performed best although only three-quarters of the responses were correct. Although the sample was very small one important finding concerned the contribution of the high ability pupils in the mixed groups. Working alongside low attainers seemed to be a positive benefit since the high attaining children were very successful at giving reasons for the decision made in the post-task interviews and made the highest contribution to instructional talk within their groups. In general on-task behaviour was high and there did appear to be links between general verbal participation and performance in the post-task interview.

In a further study by Bennett and Dunne (1989) fifteen primary teachers with classes aged between 4 and 11 years agreed to operate some of the different kinds of grouping organisation described in Chapter 1. In one group children worked individually on identical tasks with individual products, while other pupils worked individually towards a joint outcome in a jig-saw pattern. A third group worked co-operatively on a single task leading to a joint outcome. Using Piaget's (1959) classification of children's conversation a distinction was made between conversation relating to action and conversation involving abstract thought. Abstract thought centred on the ability of the participants to conduct genuine argument. In general, the evidence suggested that when the task was structured, so that children had to work together, then the level of task-related talk was much higher than in the more usual situations where children sat in groups but worked individually. Overall 88 per cent of the talk in the co-operative groups was on task compared to 66 per cent in the individualised settings.

There were also differences in the mode of talk during language work and mathematics. In mathematics talk was totally concerned with action, in contrast to language work, where nearly 25 per cent was in the abstract mode. This result came about because the tasks chosen for mathematics were mainly practical ones, involving manipulation of materials and most of the discussion was associated with demonstration while working through instructions. In language tasks children were required to evaluate different ideas for stories and the emphasis was on aspects of creative thought. Teachers who tended to set action tasks did so because during such activity talk tended to flow more easily than when more difficult abstract reasoning was involved. Talk involving abstract reasoning was often faltering compared to the spontaneity of talk relating to action and teachers often seemed to regard the latter discussions as being less worthwhile and less suitable for use with collaborative groups. The practical aspects of these findings are explored in Dunne and Bennett (1990).

Other studies, also on a very small scale have, nevertheless, tended to confirm these trends. Crozier and Kleinberg (1987) set groups of children, in the age range 7 to 11, mathematical problem-solving tasks. In one task children were shown some sums which it was said had been done by space children and which had been marked correct by their space teacher. However, in our world a teacher would have marked the same sums wrong and the children were asked to work out how the space pupils did their sums. Crozier and Kleinberg found that what Bennett and Dunn (1989) later termed the action mode was crucial in supporting group discussion. In the case of the space children's sums it helped decisions when materials were present which the children could use in talking initially about the problem. Although observations were made only on an informal basis, Crozier and Kleinberg (1987) claimed that most of the talk was on task. However, the statements made by pupils were generally assertive and were rarely challenged by the other pupils in the group. Solutions were usually arrived at on a trial and error basis rather than through reasoned argument. Interestingly most of the groups neglected to follow the instructions. Another interesting finding was that open-ended problems tended to be less helpful in stimulating collaborative discussion. In such cases where it was necessary only to find an acceptable solution, rather than the correct solution, the group tended to agree to the first suggestion put forward by one of its members. Discussion tended, therefore, to be quickly terminated.

In another study with younger children Burden et al. (1988) used logic blocks with children in groups of twos and threes. In one task the children were asked to use the logic blocks to reproduce a train of a different colour which they had to make travel in the opposite direction. Previously these groups had been mainly taught on an individualised basis although they usually sat together. Of the seven groups examined three remained very dependent on the teacher. When pupils in one of these dependent groups made a suggestion the other children tended to use them as a 'scapegoat' placing the blame on them if the teacher rejected the group solution. Burden et al. (1988) found that the situation could be improved if feedback was provided to the groups about their performance. In their research Burden et al. used the transcript of the discussion, playing back selected excerpts to the pupils who were involved. A similar conclusion was reached by

41

Glaye (1986). Video feedback was used to enable pupils to identify different retrospective task demands, using the technique of 'simulated recall' developed by Bloom (1953).

A number of studies has also been carried out examining the effectiveness of group work with micro-computers. Given the fact that there is often only one machine in a classroom the necessity of devising tasks which involve more than one pupil is essential. So far, however, such studies have often been small and artificial, in the sense that they have taken place outside the classroom. One example of this type of research is that by Fletcher (1985), who has claimed that groups of children took less time and needed to make fewer decisions to complete successfully a computer game, involving space ships, compared to children either working silently by themselves or being allowed to 'think aloud'. Currently, a much larger study is taking place examining the use of group work with computers in normal classroom conditions (Eraut and Hoyles 1989).

GENERAL CONCLUSIONS

The studies, briefly described in this chapter, vary in approach and in their methods and in their focus of interest. Nevertheless certain patterns in their findings do emerge which are generally supportive of co-operative working in the classroom. These may be summarised as follows:

1 When children sit in groups in a classroom they are likely to achieve more if they are encouraged to co-operate either by working towards a common shared outcome or by making an individual contribution towards a common goal. In the latter case part of the process should include shared decision making about the planning of these individual contributions and their combined presentation. Such groupings do seem to improve pupils' self-esteem and increase pupil motivation, as evidenced by a greater proportion of task-related conversation within such groups when compared to other forms of classroom organisation.

2 Groups function best when they are of mixed ability but such groups must include pupils from the highest ability group within the class. Where possible it should also be representative of gender and racial differences within the classroom.

There is evidence that such groups can function well with relatively low support from the teacher. A crucial factor here appears to be the teacher's ability to encourage pupils to assume overall responsibility (ownership) for the activity, thus reducing the dependency upon the teacher for approval of group decisions.

3 Children perform in different ways according to the nature of the task. Levels of conversation appear to be highest when pupils are engaged on 'action' tasks, involving practical activities where they are required either to perform or to make some object or construction. Although levels of conversation will be more sophisticated during more abstract tasks, involving, for example, a debate, such exchanges tend to be intermittent. For this reason some teachers are often reluctant to use group work for this kind of activity, feeling that it fails to generate adequate responses on the part of their pupils. While this observation is true, if judged solely by the interaction, the quality of these intermittent exchanges is often very high indeed.

4 Related to the previous finding is the fact that problem-solving tasks with a clear testable outcome tend to generate a greater degree of collaboration than more 'open-ended' tasks. The fact that there is a solution to be aimed for allows children to test out ideas and to reject those which do not satisfy the criteria for a satisfactory solution. With more 'open-ended' problems where the criteria for preferring one solution rather than another is less clear, pupils tend to be satisfied with the first solution offered. In general it appears that pupils do not like challenging each other by debating the value of each other's solutions. They tend to assert rather than to hypothesise or raise questions in this kind of discussion.

5 For successful collaboration to take place pupils need to be taught how to collaborate so that they have a clear idea of what is expected of them. In this process the need for immediate feedback followed by further discussion with the teacher appears crucial.

6 There remains considerable doubt about the value of building in individual rewards within the collaborative exercise so that pupils who perform best receive recognition. One possible way of reconciling the different evidence on this point is to regard group work as a two-stage process, the initial and

subsequent encounters requiring the use of different strategies by the teacher.

The above findings offer considerable reassurance to those advocates of group work. It not only appears to be a device for overcoming logistical problems within the modern primary class-room but also appears to have considerable cognitive benefits for pupils of different ability, gender and race. There remain, how-ever, considerable problems to be solved, largely because the researchers ignored the theoretical perspectives developed by social psychologists which were discussed in the final part of the previous chapter. Although some of these studies described have measured classroom environment and pupil self-esteem this has been done in very general terms and in ways which do not allow the results to be interpreted with any confidence in regard to the importance of this measure. As demonstrated by Kutnick (1988) self-esteem is a composite measure derived partly through academic success and partly through peer relationships and it appears to function in different ways for pupils with different ability.

The importance of the concept in helping teachers devise effec-tive strategies for implementing collaborative group work may be deduced from the findings stating that the degree of collaboration differs within different task settings. In particular the finding that the more complex the task, in the sense that there is greater ambiguity about what is expected of the pupil, the greater the risk attached to offering solutions, (Doyle 1986) suggests that pupils' self-concepts are crucial if they are to take on the 'ownership' of the activity and so run the groups on their own. In all the studies listed in this chapter there is little attempt to gather the perceptions of the pupils about their experience of working in groups as opposed to other forms of classroom organisation. One study (Cullingford 1988) does record pupils' reactions to working collaboratively but we are given very little data to judge the context in which their remarks were made nor do we know what proportion of pupils in Cullingford's sample were responding so positively.

The second weakness of research on collaborative grouping is that it offers very little guidance to teachers about their role in the process. There is in some research vague references to teachers as 'facilitators' or as 'negotiators' but just what this involves is rarely discussed. Yet any teacher who has attempted to instigate group work in their classroom will readily testify to the fact that one of their major dilemmas concerns when to intervene and when not to intervene within a group. In clarifying the nature and in establishing the effectiveness of these interactions between teachers and pupils during collaborative group work the findings from social psychology, presented in the first chapter are, therefore, also likely to be of relevance.

Thus the findings testifying to the cognitive benefits of group work need to be set within a wider context which acknowledges the different social settings which operate in the classroom and need to identify the expectation about the roles which each of the participants thinks they are required to play. We need to know what pupils expect of their teachers during group work and what teachers expect of their pupils because behind these expectations lie implicit theories about how groups are perceived to function. In this way we may hope to build a more comprehensive theory of how groups can function effectively in the primary classroom. It is this question which we now seek to address and in the next two chapters we describe the work of the ORACLE project and subsequent research which has, over a decade, explored some of the issues discussed in the previous pages.

3

GROUP WORK IN THE ORACLE STUDY

The pupils' perspective

THE NATURE OF THE ORACLE RESEARCH

This chapter tells a story of how, starting with the ORACLE (Observational Research and Classroom Learning Evaluation) Project which took place during the period 1975–80 studies of classroom practice at the University of Leicester have increasingly focused on the problems associated with the inter-action of pupils and teachers within collaborative settings. There are parallels here with Bennett's (1985) admission of moving towards the same focus over the same period. Whereas, however, Bennett and his research team have focused primarily on cognitive aspects of the interactions and the context under which these interactions become more effective, researchers at Leicester have increasingly turned their attention on the way in which pupils within collaborative settings create their social identity and how this affects the learning process. In this we are supported by other researchers such as Burns (1989) who queries the fact that the third edition of the *Handbook of Research on Teaching* (Wittrock 1986), for example, 'contains no entry in the appendix for key constructs within the socio-emotional reflective dimensions such as self-esteem and self-concept'. Burns (1989: 28) argues that:

> Teachers (and children) are not merely factors in the system or passive agents in an instructional process. Teachers (and children) adjust to the social environment of a classroom in much the same ways as they adjust to the social environment outside the classroom. They display the same modes of coping, the same strengths and the same weaknesses.

According to Burns, therefore, any analysis of teaching which does not take into account the fundamental social elements of classroom life is, at best, an incomplete one. An approach of the kind suggested by Burns is complimentary to the research described in the previous chapter, in that by focusing more directly on the teachers' and pupils' perceptions about working in groups it can offer explanations for certain of the findings summarised at the conclusion of the previous chapter. For example some of the research described so far has supported the finding that talk was more prolific when it involved a practical activity rather than an abstract one such as that which takes place during a debate or a discussion. This research does not, however, offer explanations as to why this should be so nor does it help teachers who may still wish to encourage children to engage in abstract reasoning within group discussion. Another crucial area seems to revolve around the question of 'ownership' of the task. The research findings seem to indicate that it is difficult to persuade children to break out of the 'dependent' mode in which they continually seek the teacher's approval for their group decisions. Some explanation for this conclusion is also necessary if teachers are to be able to devise satisfactory strategies to overcome the problem.

THE ORACLE PROJECT AND GROUP WORK

First, however, we shall examine the data collected during the main ORACLE study, much of it descriptive, but which helped to focus the direction of subsequent work. The ORACLE Project, the first major observational study of the British primary classroom, took place over a five-year period from 1975 to 1980. One of its main aims was to describe the effectiveness of different styles of teaching and their effects upon pupil behaviour and on pupil achievement. Pupils were observed with different teachers, in most cases for two years, and in some cases for three, so that the extent to which pupil behaviour and achievement was replicated across different classrooms where similar styles of teaching were used could be studied.

Mention has already been made in Chapter 1 (p. 11) of one of the major findings of the project, described as 'the asymmetry' of classroom interaction. Because, in general, the preferred teaching strategy was setting specific tasks to individual pupils, the most frequent kind of interaction carried out by teachers was to engage in exchanges with one pupil at a time. These exchanges were of very short duration and mostly consisted of providing information or giving routine managerial instructions, designed to facilitate the completion of the task. Typically teachers spent around 80 per cent of the day engaged in these kinds of interactions. In contrast pupils spent nearly 80 per cent of their day working on their own with the teacher engaged elsewhere in the classroom. When pupils were seated in groups, the usual practice, approximately 20 per cent of the time when the pupil was not involved with the teacher was spent interacting with other pupils (i.e. 20 per cent of 80 per cent). However, two-thirds of these conversations were non-task related. During the remaining 20 per cent of the time, when the teacher was not engaged in giving individual attention to pupils, approximately 9.5 per cent of these observations involved the teacher talking with a group of pupils.

These figures, however, masked a wide range of behaviour. In a separate survey, during which observers were asked to record the incidence of children working in groups on a common task, it was found that 69 per cent of teachers in the sample never used any kind of co-operative group work for either art and craft or topic work and nearly 90 per cent never did so with single subject teaching such as mathematics and language. This led to the conclusion that group work was therefore a relatively 'neglected art' in the primary classroom (Galton 1981).

The PRISMS project, concerning curriculum provision in small schools, also provided some interesting findings regarding the use of group work across different curriculum areas. Where the teacher's audience was a group of pupils this was more likely to occur when the topic involved language and was less likely to involve mathematics and science in any significant degree. However, examination of the kinds of language interactions indicated that these were likely to consist of listening to statements about the content of the task or to routine instructions to deal with the procedures associated with the task. In the main, therefore, the function of these groups was to make it easier for teachers to convey instructions.

These findings from the PRISMS study confirmed the teaching styles analysis carried out during the ORACLE Project. One of the ORACLE styles was called the *Group Instructor* because it highlighted the very same interactions displayed by teachers in the PRISMS study whenever they were involved with groups of children rather than individuals or the whole class. These ORACLE teachers, about 12 per cent of the sample, tended to emphasise factual and routine statements, compared with presentation of ideas but they also, by working through groups rather than with individuals, provided higher levels of feedback. The observers' descriptions of such teachers told of their concern to structure the work of a group carefully before leaving them to carry on the tasks among themselves. Once all the groups had begun work the teacher would rejoin an earlier group and respond to pupils' ideas and solutions by providing feedback. Although there was some evidence of problem solving, the main emphasis of these teachers' styles was on the informational aspects of their teaching. As a result they were therefore labelled *group instructors*.

What is of interest to the present discussion was the correspondence between the particular teaching style and the pupils' behaviour. When pupils were taught by *group instructors* they tended to engage in higher levels of group interaction than pupils taught by any other style. However, the majority of these pupil–pupil exchanges were non-verbal, hence the groups were called the *quiet collaborators*. The highest proportion of interactions involved pupils sharing materials and the observers' accounts showed that such activities usually involved drawing maps, making measurements and constructing models. This finding is closely related to the research discussed in the previous chapter. There it was found that group collaboration tended to improve when it was organised around 'action' tasks of a practical nature and that teachers appeared to favour these kinds of activities, rather than more abstract tasks involving discussion, because they resulted in higher levels of on-task co-operative activity.

The ORACLE study, however, offered a more intriguing explanation for this practice. Several of the observers' accounts appeared to suggest that it was the pupils rather than the teacher who determined the nature of the group activity. In many cases pupils were encouraged by the teacher to share ideas, prior to engaging in the practical activity. In most of these instances, however, it was observed that the pupils tended to ignore the teacher's instructions when required, for example, first to discuss which pupil should colour in various sections of a map. Instead pupils would proceed immediately to the practical activity, assuming responsibility for different tasks on a 'first-come-first-served' basis. Discussion would then, as also reported by Bennett and Dunne (1989), consist mainly of low-level exchanges of the kind, 'Can I have the blue pencil?' or 'What colour are you using to do the main roads?'. Where teachers did attempt to insist on extended discussion, prior to beginning the practical task, pupils would tend to increase the amount of off-task, disruptive behaviour which would cause the teacher either to abandon the activity or to acquiesce to the pupil's desire to move on quickly to the practical work.

Under such conditions, therefore, a kind of 'covert' form of negotiation appeared to take place. Pupils seemed willing to work co-operatively provided they were not required to engage in extensive discussions among themselves while doing so. Where teachers insisted on prior discussion then pupils would engage in the kind of behaviour that they knew would either provoke the teacher to abandon the task or persuade her to allow pupils to engage in the activity in ways which they deemed more acceptable. Put another way, these pupils seemed to be saying to the teacher, 'If we can do this group activity in the way that we find acceptable then we will behave in ways which you will find acceptable'.

ORACLE II: EFFECTIVE GROUP WORK IN THE PRIMARY CLASSROOM

Following the completion of the ORACLE Project in 1980 it seemed clear that further research was required into the teacher's use of group work strategies in the classroom. At the time the research team's interest in the topic centred mainly on the need for more effective classroom management strategies on the part of teachers rather than on any consideration of the cognitive and social benefits for the pupils. The ORACLE study clearly demonstrated the problematic nature of much current classroom practice which, for the most part, required teachers either to move rapidly around the classroom dealing with the requests of upwards of twenty-five children (a typical sized classroom in the ORACLE study) or to sit at a desk while a queue of pupils formed to await attention. The PRISMS study (Galton and Patrick 1990) subsequently showed not only that most of these exchanges were limited to giving information and dealing with managerial concerns, but also they were of very short duration. In the PRISMS research, using a five-second time interval between observations, note was taken of whether the teacher was still interacting with the same pupil as at the previous time signal. From the analysis it was estimated that around 40 per cent of all exchanges between teachers and pupils did not last five seconds. Hence the limited amount of extended discussion concerned with higher level cognitive activity. Faced with these problems it seemed important to inquire why so little use was made of collaborative group work which, in theory, allowed teachers to deal with groups of children instead of individuals and which also allowed peer-tutoring to take place within the groups, cutting down the need for the teacher to engage constantly in low level cognitive interactions such as checking answers, explaining instructions, or indicating where necessary equipment could be found.

The strategy adopted for ORACLE II or, as it came to be called, 'Son of ORACLE' was first to conduct a postal questionnaire survey of all schools in the three local authorities in which the first ORACLE Project had been carried out. In ORACLE I only a small number of schools was involved because, even with ten observers, it was possible to obtain a reasonable sample of teacher and pupil behaviour in a maximum of only sixty-five classes per year. As part of the research involved the study of transfer, in some cases more than one teacher was observed in a particular school. This was because all classes of pupils in the feeder school who would transfer to the secondary school in the subsequent year were observed. It was possible, therefore, that among the majority of schools, in a local authority where no observation took place, there were teachers who used above average amounts of collaborative group work in their classrooms.

The second stage of the new research was to visit classrooms where teachers, identified from the questionnaire, engaged in collaborative group work and to observe their practice as a check that what these teachers believed was happening was in fact taking place. Having confirmed that collaborative group work was indeed being used, the third stage of the project was to ask these teachers to devise a programme of in-service work which would enable other teachers to develop similar practices in their classrooms. This latter group of teachers was to be selected at random from a larger sample which had volunteered to take part in the study. Some of the remaining teachers, who were not selected for this in-service programme, were then to act as a control group in an experiment of the kind carried out by American researchers which was described in the previous chapter.

The ORACLE II research design had several novel features. First it attempted to carry out the recommendation of Rosenshine and Furst (1973) that classroom research should proceed by means of a correlation–experimental loop – that is that descriptive studies should first establish key variables in the process of teacher effectiveness and then manipulate these variables in a true experimental design (Campbell and Stanley 1963). In a true experiment all factors, other than the one under investigation, are controlled in both the experimental group (the one receiving the new treatment) and the control group. Any change in the dependent variable (in this case the pupils' behaviour and their attainment) could then, in theory, be attributed to the change in treatment received by the experimental group. The use of such experimental designs to study teaching effectiveness was, however, at the time the subject of some controversy (Parlett and Hamilton 1976). It was argued that such designs were artificial in the sense that the conditions created to ensure that the experiment had 'internal validity' (that is efficient control over all other variables within the study so that the performance of the pupils could be ascribed only to the treatment they received) were at the cost of 'external validity' (that is the pupils were then taught in a way and under conditions which differed appreciably from that normally experienced within their classroom).

In an attempt to overcome this criticism it was decided that an 'action research' approach (shown in Figure 3.1) would be adopted during the in-service training programme. The form of 'action research' was similar to that developed by Elliott (1976) and his colleagues and involved teachers working alongside consultants within their own classroom to develop and change practice in ways which were congruent with their intentions. Thus the plan was for the 'expert' teachers who had already demonstrated 'above average' competence in the use of collaborative group work to act as consultants to other teachers within the programme. The practice which developed would then be of a kind which matched the demands of a particular classroom situation and a particular school context although the criteria for satisfactory practice, namely the effective use of collaborative

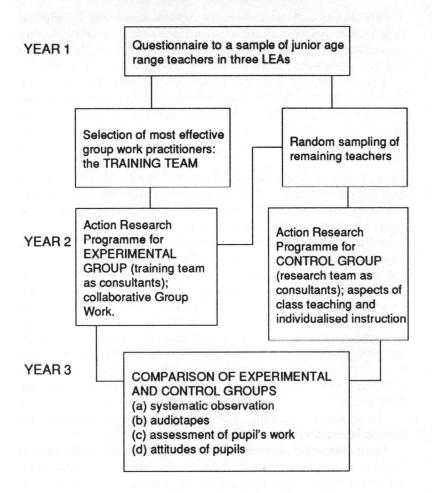

YEAR 1 — Questionnaire to a sample of junior age range teachers in three LEAs

Selection of most effective group work practitioners: the TRAINING TEAM

Random sampling of remaining teachers

YEAR 2 — Action Research Programme for EXPERIMENTAL GROUP (training team as consultants); collaborative Group Work.

Action Research Programme for CONTROL GROUP (research team as consultants); aspects of class teaching and individualised instruction

YEAR 3 — COMPARISON OF EXPERIMENTAL AND CONTROL GROUPS
(a) systematic observation
(b) audiotapes
(c) assessment of pupil's work
(d) attitudes of pupils

Figure 3.1 Plan of ORACLE II study: effective group work in the primary classroom

group work, would be the same in all cases. On paper the plan looked both pleasing and feasible and the research team was confident that it could obtain satisfactory results within the three-year period of the project. A decade later, and with the researchers considerably wiser, it is now clear that developing effective group work in the primary classroom constitutes a more formidable challenge.

This brief historical overview is important not only in helping to chart the progress of the research but also in relation to the subsequent discussion in Chapter 8 concerning the INSET activity, designed to improve levels of collaborative working in schools. Within Chapter 8 the concept of the action research approach will be discussed and certain modifications suggested as the result of experience gained during ORACLE II.

THE GROUP WORK QUESTIONNAIRE

The questionnaire was sent to a one in three sample of primary and middle schools in the three local authorities where the original ORACLE I study was conducted. Out of 225 schools sampled 149 responded, a 66 per cent return. In the city area of local authority A only lower schools (5–9) were included and in local authority C only middle schools (9–13) were sampled. Within the 149 schools the teachers of the junior age range were invited to fill in questionnaires, giving a return of 770 responses for analysis. The sample consisted of 34 per cent men; 47 per cent of teachers were in the age range 25–34; 35 per cent had been in their present school under two years; 24 per cent between three and five years and the further 23 per cent for between six and eight years; 71 per cent of the sample had engaged in in-service training, consisting of at least five sessions, during the previous three years.

The pattern of organisation within the classroom, adopted by these teachers, showed considerable flexibility. When sequencing activities just under half the teachers tended to have all pupils working in the same subject area at the same time for the largest part of the day. Grouping policies, however, varied considerably. Over two-thirds of the teachers tended to group pupils either in mixed ability groups or by allowing pupils who worked well together to sit together or by letting pupils have free choice of where to sit.

The main part of the questionnaire, however, concerned the teachers' practice during a typical day. Twenty different classroom practices were listed and teachers were asked to say whether they had used them on the particular day in question. The format of this question was constructed around the distinction made by Elliott as a result of the Ford Teaching Study. In constructing a typology of teaching styles Elliott (1978) distinguished between teacher control of the product and of control of the processes by which the pupil worked towards the production of this outcome. At its simplest these teacher-researchers argued that it would be of limited use for the teacher to tell pupils that they were free to choose how to find a solution to the problem if, in the same breath, the pupils were told that whatever solution was adopted it must be capable of being written on an A4 size piece of paper so that it could be read by other pupils in the class. Teachers were asked about the choice of activities or themes, the extent to which discussion about the activity took place either as a whole class or in groups and whether the theme of discussion was one chosen by the teacher or by the pupils. Respondents were asked whether the choice of working method was specified by the teacher either verbally or by means of work sheets or whether it was chosen by the group of pupils and whether the outcome consisted of a jointly finished product on which pupils co-operated or whether individual contributions were required from each pupil.

The results demonstrated that the teachers' perceptions of their activities was broadly in agreement with the observations carried out during the ORACLE I project; 72 per cent of teachers' interactions were with individuals, 19 per cent were with the whole class and 9 per cent with small groups. Of the twenty classroom practices surveyed, seven represented some kind of collaborative activity ranging from co-operative group work where children worked in groups but on individual assignments to collaborative working where a jointly finished piece of work resulted and pupils were able to choose not only the theme but also the method of working. Of the teachers, 18 per cent never engaged in any of the seven practices and only 18 per cent in more than half the seven. The majority of these teachers tended to favour discussion in groups on a theme which was chosen by the teacher in which, after the discussion, the pupils were required to produce an individual product. The links between the aims of teachers and their practice appeared to be weak. Teachers who placed a very high importance on independent judgement were rather more likely to make use of group work but a large number of teachers who supported this aim gave pupils little choice in the arrangement of their own work. Further when the teachers who had the highest proportions of group practices were visited and observed informally, using the categories of the Observation

Schedule developed by Boydell (1975) for the first ORACLE Project, there was a marked absence of sustained pupil–pupil interaction within these groups whenever the teacher was elsewhere in the classroom.

In the first ORACLE Project sustained interaction between pupils was said to have taken place if the same pair or group of pupils were continuing to talk (even intermittently) over a time interval of 25 seconds. There it was shown that although 18.6 per cent of the pupils' time was spent interacting with other pupils less than a third of these exchanges was sustained and, of these extended conversations over 80 per cent were not concerned with the task. It appeared from informal observations of a similar kind in ORACLE II that although some teachers (less than a fifth of the whole sample) were strongly committed to the aims associated with group work and organised their classes so that it could take place, there was very little evidence that their aims were successfully implemented when groups of pupils were left to work independently.

THE GROUP WORK EXPERIMENT

This finding presented an immediate problem for the research team since it was no longer possible to implement the original research design, whereby a group of successful practitioners would conduct an in-service programme for other teachers who wished to implement group work strategies in their classrooms. The plan was therefore revised (as shown in Figure 3.2) to include a two-stage action research programme. In stage one a group of teachers drawn from the sample in local authority B, who were strongly committed to collaborative group work, took part in a programme in which the research team acted as consultants. The aim of this programme was to investigate ways of raising the level of pupil–pupil interaction within the groups and the quality of this interaction. This process occupied the first two terms of the second year of the project. In the summer term these teachers worked in groups developing an INSET programme for the experimental group of teachers which could take place in the following autumn. At the same time the experimental group would work alongside these INSET providers who now acted as consultants. The themes chosen for the in-service programme involved investigations of ways into group work, improving

classroom organisation, identifying skills and devising procedures for monitoring and evaluating the group activities.

A parallel in-service programme was devised for the control
group of teachers. This was conducted by the research team and
focused on other aspects of the ORACLE I research which were
designed to introduce the more successful teaching styles (such
as infrequent changers and class enquirers) into the repertoire of
strategies used in the classroom.

The net result of all these changes in the research plan was a
considerable reduction in the time available to conduct the
experiment during the third year of the research. Bearing in mind

YEAR 2 (terms one and two)	Invitation of volunteer teachers from Local Authority B to participate in one year's ACTION RESEARCH programme on collaborative group work (research team as consultants)
YEAR 2 (third term)	Creation of training programme for experimental study based upon four units (a) ways into group work (b) organisation (c) identification of skills and (d) monitoring and evaluation
YEAR 3 (term one first half term two)	New group of schools selected for experimental study: in each school pairs of teachers are randomly assigned to *either* (a) group work training programme *or* (b) improving class discussion and individualised instruction
YEAR 3 (second half term two)	Comparison of pupils in the experimental and control pairs of classrooms as in original study: each pair teaches same theme or topic

Figure 3.2 Revised plan for ORACLE II experiment

57

the criticisms made of Johnson and Johnson's (1976) studies it was originally hoped to conduct observations of classroom practice in the experimental and control classrooms and to assess pupil performance over at least two terms and across a number of curriculum areas. Now there was time for only one study of a month's duration. Where it was possible the teachers in the experimental and control groups were matched in pairs, in terms of school type (open plan, box classroom, school, size) and by age of the pupils taught. In the majority of pairs the experimental teacher and the control teacher came from the same school and taught parallel classes. Each pair of teachers was asked to choose a theme which involved work in as many curriculum areas as possible. The experimental member of the pair organised this work in collaborative groups whereas the control teacher used class discussion followed by individual work in seated groups.

Pupils were observed with a modified form of pupil record during the first and the third week of the programme. The teacher's introduction to the topic was taped, as also was one example of a discussion which took place between groups of children. At the end of the evaluation attitudes of children were measured using a series of cartoon pictures representing different classroom practices. Pupils were asked to express their like or dislike for certain kinds of activities and to write down what they thought the pupils in the picture were saying to each other. At the end of the month the children's topic work was collected and a note was taken of whether the product was a joint effort or consisted of individual contributions. The teachers who had provided the INSET programme and had acted as consultants to the experimental group were then to be asked to rate this work, without knowing from which classroom it had been collected.

The results from the first systematic observation were most encouraging. The proportion of lessons involving sustained discussion (lasting beyond the 25 seconds) was 35 per cent in the experimental group compared to 19.2 per cent in the control although the teacher was present in groups for approximately the same amount of time in both the experimental and the control classrooms (11.4 per cent compared to 10.4 per cent). The degree of distraction and the time spent waiting for teachers were all marginally lower in the experimental groups compared to the control groups. However, two weeks later most of these differences had disappeared. While extended discussion in the control groups remained at just under 20 per cent that in the experimental group had dropped to 24.6 per cent. The degree of distraction had risen in both groups to around 18 per cent of all task activity and there was increased teacher involvement in the experimental group.

Faced with these findings the experiment had to be abandoned. There was little point in trying to assess the performance of pupils in the experimental group and compare this with their controls when it had been demonstrated that there were no differences in the pattern and quantity of the interactions taking place among children who were working in groups and those who, while sitting in groups, were working individually. The observation data were, therefore, re-examined to see if they offered some clue as to why the original burst of collaborative activity within the experimental group had not been sustained.

When the first set of observations was examined the most significant difference between the experimental group and the control group was in the nature of the activity which was associated with group discussion. Nearly 71 per cent of all such observations involved use of materials compared to only 40 per cent in the control group. This raised the possibility that differences in the curriculum area covered by the topic were associated with the level of extended discussion within the groups of pupils. This hypothesis was confirmed when correlation coefficients, showing the association between the amount of group discussion and the curriculum area featured in the topic work, were calculated. In the experimental group discussion was negatively correlated with reading (−0.129), writing (−0.385), measuring (−0.351) and arithmetic computation (−0.278). It was however positively correlated with the use of materials (0.541). When a similar procedure was carried out for the control group the same pattern was obtained. The reason why the experimental group had shown higher levels of extended discussion during the first round of systematic observation was, therefore, because they were engaged in activities which required greater use of shared materials and hence a greater degree of collaboration. Once the topic was underway, however, and the pupils were making less use of materials and either writing up results or collecting information by reading reference books then the pattern of working in both the experimental and the control groups tended to be very similar. Pupils exhibited similar behaviours to those

59

observed in the first ORACLE study where there were high levels of distraction whenever children sat in groups but were working individually on such activities. These results are similar to those, discussed in the last chapter, where Bennett and Dunne (1989) and Crozier and Kleinberg (1987) both reported that the frequency of group interaction was far higher when it consisted of 'action' talk related to shared practical activities but that only intermittent discussion occurred when more abstract discussion involving ideas took place, as, for example, when children were discussing among themselves what to write or how to solve a mathematical problem.

PUPILS' ATTITUDES TO GROUP WORK

Given that pupil behaviour was highly correlated with the nature of the subject matter in which pupils were engaged, the examination of pupils' attitudes towards these various activities within different classroom settings was clearly of interest. When the research team had orginally discussed the value of including an attitudinal measure within the research plan a number of problems presented themselves. Foremost among these was the repeated finding that the level of attitude often did not correlate highly with behaviour. Many reasons have been advanced for this discrepancy, one of which is of particular concern here. This is the phenomenon known as 'agreed response bias' where the respondents provide answers which they feel the designer of the questionnaire wants rather than those which they feel best expresses their own beliefs and values. This can be a particularly acute problem when attitude inventories are used. For example, in the 1960s there were a number of studies of student teachers where researchers wished to find out whether the attitudes changed during the college course. It was found that the student teachers' attitudes became more liberal as the course progressed so that, in general, they supported a 'child-centred' approach. However, other studies showed that when students were asked to fill in the attitude inventory in a way which would display either a 'conservative' or a 'liberal' attitude, they had no difficulty in doing so. This raised the possibility that students filled in the inventory in the way they did, not because they believed in 'child-centredness' but because the College of Education did and the student teachers, for various reasons, did not wish to display

attitudes which were contrary to the college philosophy. Consequently, much attitude research has concerned ways of
encouraging respondents to reveal their real beliefs and values by
creating situations where they were not aware of the purpose of
the exercise. In the case of primary-aged pupils, where the urge to
please the teacher can be very strong, there were therefore
dangers in using any kind of attitude inventory which asked
questions about which classroom practice the children preferred.

Rejection of the questionnaire approach to attitude measurement leads to a different concept of what an attitude is. Those
who use questionnaires as the basis for determining attitudes
view an attitude as 'a disposition to act in a certain way'. Some
social psychologists such as Madga Arnold (1962) have
questioned the assumption that an attitude is 'a readiness for
action'. She suggests that it is possible to be well disposed
towards something, for example religion, without feeling it
necessary to attend church each Sunday. She therefore argues
that we need to distinguish between two kinds of attitude, *evaluative* attitudes and *motivating* attitudes. For Arnold a value is
based upon a judgement that something is desirable whereas a
motive requires in addition a choice of action. As long as values
are not accompanied by an appraisal for action they do not influence behaviour. When they are, however, they become motives.
Attitudes develop when either values or motives become
habitual. According to Arnold an evaluative attitude consists of
habitual values and a motivating attitude of habitual motives.
Evaluative attitudes cannot therefore be used to predict action
(Arnold 1962: 42). To distinguish between these different types of
attitudes Arnold makes use of Morgan and Murray's (1935)
Thematic Apperception Test (TAT). According to Murray individuals are likely to reveal their motivation while interpreting
pictures showing ambiguous social situations. In essence Morgan
and Murray argued that through such mechanisms as projection
and identification with the characters in the story a person is able
to reveal aspects of self which govern the development of values
and motives.

Over the years there has been considerable debate about this
proposition (Warren and Jahoda 1976). A number of studies
showed that the strength of people's drive was not always
reflected in their projections. For example, Arnold cites Sandford
et al.'s (1943) reported finding that the number of aggressive

themes in TAT stories of aggressive adolescence was the same as in the stories of well-adjusted boys. Arnold herself argues that the problem arises because the pictures are considered in isolation and that motivating attitudes, that is the ones that are predictors of action, can be determined only when account is taken of the plot and the outcome of the whole story. Of importance to this present study, however, is that there is general agreement that whatever the problems of determining motivating attitudes, such pictures do reveal an attitude component particularly when they are used not just to tell a story but to express preferences so that respondents not only have to describe what is happening in the picture but also, subsequently, to express their preference for one situation rather than another. The technique has been used in this way by McClelland (1963) to explore the characteristics of eminent scientists and by Hudson (1966) in a study of the personality characteristics of secondary school pupils who opted either for arts or science specialism.

One problem in interpreting the response to TAT pictures is the variation in length of the responses made by different individuals. In a story depicting, for example, aggressive behaviour, the longer the response the more instances of aggression are likely to be found. This will be a particular problem with primary-aged children, where during written composition one pupil in a class may complete a page of writing while another can produce only three lines. Accordingly, during the development of cartoon pictures to use in the present study, various forms of presentation were tried out during the pilot stage. The simplest, to include 'speech bubbles' in the cartoon, was quickly abandoned because it often produced only a one-word response consisting of exclamations such as 'ugh!' or 'aah!' Free response was also rejected because in most cases it produced only two lines of dialogue between pupils. Eventually the following format was adopted.

The picture shows a group of children at work in a classroom. Write down what two of these pupils are saying to each other.

Pupil 1   . . .
Pupil 2   . . .
Pupil 1   . . .
Pupil 2   . . .

If the teacher is present you should decide whether the teacher or the pupils are talking. If the teacher is talking write down what he/she is saying.

Teacher   . . .

The actual cartoons were drawn by some of the consultant teachers to the experimental group. As far as possible, the features of the characters in each cartoon were made expressionless lest, for example, a teacher depicted with a smiling face might trigger responses indicating positive effect. In later studies (Cavendish 1988) where attitudes of male and female pupils towards mathematics were studied, more professionally produced pictures were designed and examples of these are shown in Figure 3.3. In this case the positions and sex of the pupils and teachers could be rearranged to provide different environments. In a more recent study the technique has been employed with children in the reception class with the cartoon pictures replaced by a 'play classroom'. The 5 year old children were asked to tell the interviewer what is happening in the 'play classroom' that they had made. The important point is that whatever procedure is adopted the patterns of responses are remarkably similar, indicating a certain degree of robustness and reliability in the method.

In the ORACLE II study, twelve pictures were constructed. Each picture showed five pupils seated around the table. The pupils were shown at work on one of four activities.

1 Doing art work using a variety of materials but each pupil shown with an individual sheet of paper.
2 Writing on individual sheets of paper.
3 Discussing with a tape recorder at the centre of a table.
4 Collaborating together in measuring a drawing on a large sheet of paper.

Pictures 1 and 2 therefore depicted what in Chapter 1 was termed working groups, whereas pictures 3 and 4 depicted collaborative groups in which the pupils were working on a joint outcome. For each of the four activities three different teacher positions were shown. In the first position, no teacher appeared in the picture, while in the second position the teacher had joined the group at the table. In the third position the teacher was shown standing near a blackboard addressing the whole class. Combining teacher position and the four activities thus produced twelve pictures in

Figure 3.3 Sequence of cartoon pictures used to study gender differences in attitudes to mathematics (a) teacher–individual pupil (b) group work teacher present (c) incomplete picture.

all. The gender of the teacher in the picture was altered according to whether the class teacher was a man or a women. Of the five pupils in the group, three were boys and two were girls.

The comments of the pupils were most revealing. Nearly all the conversations between pupils were of the kind labelled by Bennett and Dunne (1989) as 'action' talk in which pupils asked for information about what to do next or else sought confirmation that what they had already done was correct. Typical of the exchanges was the following.

Pupil 1   I've finished.
Pupil 2   You've done it wrong.
Pupil 1   No I haven't. The teacher told us to do it this way.

In all, just over two-thirds of all these exchanges concerned getting work right or wrong. In over 50 per cent of these instances the teacher was mentioned in the dialogue as, for example, 'You've got that wrong. Take it to the teacher.' Where the teacher was present in the cartoon he or she was nearly always perceived to be talking rather than listening. In these cases the large proportion of the teacher's comments were to do with admonishment for bad behaviour or exhortation for the pupils to improve. 'Get on' or 'That's wrong. Do it again' were typical. In other cases the teacher was presented as a resource either offering information or giving directions. 'London is the capital of England', or 'The pencils are in the cupboard', provide two illustrative examples of this kind of utterance. Similar patterns were found in Cavendish's study. She carried out a content analysis of responses and these are shown in Table 3.1. In Cavendish's study the stimulus consisted of a sentence

A boy (girl) has all his work wrong. The teacher is saying . . .

Typical of the completions would be statements such as 'Do it again and this time concentrate', or 'Think again and read the exercise properly'. Cavendish scored these responses into sixteen descriptive categories. Table 3.1 compares the results of the content analysis for the above sentence (column 3) with the open-ended response (column 1) to the sentence 'One of the girls (boys) is saying . . .' while column 2 shows the content analysis resulting from the sentence 'The girl (boy) has all her work right. The teacher is saying . . .'.

Table 3.1 Pupils' frequency of response to sentence completion task
(Cavendish 1988)

	Category	Sentence topic		
No	Classification	Open ended	Getting sums right	Getting sums wrong
1	Inform routine	16	18	17
2	Enquire routine	24	8	1
3	Inform non-task routine	15	25	3
4	Difficulty/dislike	63	53	0
5	Enquire non-task	62	71	1
6	Praise behaviour	0	1	1
7	Praise/liking	30	46	1
8	Give non-fact, info-task	10	17	73
9	Corrective behaviour	8	23	204
10	Ask fact, info-task	64	24	27
11	Give fact, info-task	33	32	5
12	Praise task work	3	3	23
13	Corrective task	9	12	5
14	Other task related	8	12	3
15	Ask non-fact, info-task	35	24	7
16	Nastiness/scorn	6	17	0
	TOTALS	386	386	386

The most noticeable feature of Table 3.1 is the strong association in the pupils' minds between getting the sums wrong and receiving criticism for behaviour. Statements such as

'Disgraceful'
'Pay attention next time.'

were commonplace accounting for 53 per cent of all responses to this statement. The next highest category (19 per cent) occurred where teachers provided information on the task by way of feedback such as

'Do it again. This time multiply.'

In contrast the responses to the other two sentences were much more evenly distributed. The first column showing the responses to the open-ended sentence shows a high incidence of exchanging factual information. Together these categories (code 10, 11 and 15) sum to 34 per cent of all responses to the statement. In the second column where pupils are responding to another member of the group getting the sums right the highest category of responses centres around liking and disliking (category code 4 and 7) accounting for 26 per cent followed by non-task discussions (category code 5) at 18 per cent. Dislike and liking tended to be gender related. If a girl got her work right the boy would say 'smart Alec' or 'girls are always brainless' whereas a female pupil would respond 'very well done. I got mine right too'. Girls were equally hard on boys. When the boy got the work right the girl would say 'creep' but another male pupil would say 'good kid'.

These exchanges provide added support for the validity of the method, particularly given the responses in column 1 where the emphasis on factual, routine and task exchanges of information typify the findings from the first ORACLE study. There is also little evidence in all these statements of abstract talk of the kind described in the previous chapter. Most importantly, the correspondence between these statements and observations of classroom practice suggest that the attitudes represented are motivational in the sense used by Arnold (1962).

A feature of these responses, together with those described earlier, covering a wider range of subjects, is the strong association between failure on task and being criticised for behaviour. In turn this appears to create apprehension in the minds of the pupils, what John Holt (1984) eloquently describes as 'fear of failure'. This is typified by one pupil's description of the cartoon picture in Cavendish's research.

> The classroom with chidren in the class are trying to lern how to do somes. The feel nerves and skared incase they get it wrong and they are trying to imagin about there work.

Returning to the question of preferences for certain types of activity in the ORACLE II, the first choices of 578 pupils from 20 classes where the cartoons were administered are shown in Table 3.2. There it can be seen that over 50 per cent of children's first preferences concerned sharing materials but then working on their own to produce an individual product (a picture). The other

Table 3.2 Pupils' first preferences of twelve 'cartoon' pictures of the primary classroom (expressed as per cent of 728 responses)

Pupil Activity	Teachers' role			Totals
	Teacher present	Teacher absent	Class instruction	
Writing individually	5	4	7	16
Working individually (composing a picture but sharing materials)	19	17	14	50
Making measurements in a group	6	8	4	18
Discussing in a group	5	4	7	16
Totals	35	33	32	100

picture combinations were all equally popular although to a markedly less degree each of the combinations accounting for around 16 per cent of the total preferences. Across the different arrangements where the teacher was either present in the group, or absent (presumably with another group) or monitoring or instructing the whole class, no overall pattern emerged. Approximately a third of the pupils indicated a preference for one of these arrangements and this pattern was consistent across all the tasks. When children were asked which situation they least liked two pictures were rejected more than others. The least popular picture (17 per cent) was the one where pupils were tape recording a discussion and the second least popular was when they were engaged in writing. In both cases the teacher was not present. Only 4 per cent of the pupils rejected the most popular picture where children were engaged in individual art work with the teacher present. The remaining nine pictures were rejected by between 6 per cent and 9 per cent of pupils.

Because of the low number of preferences for some of the pictures there were some classes where no choices existed for a particular cartoon. It was therefore not possible to carry out a full analysis of class differences with respect to each of the twelve pictures. Two separate analyses were therefore performed, one where the teacher position varied, neglecting differences in activity, and the other for differences in activity neglecting teacher position. Choices and rejections were analysed separately and although there were some differences between classes, particularly in respect of the question of whether the teacher was or was not present and whether the activity was class discussion, these differences were not a function of whether the class belonged to the experimental or to the control group.

PUPILS' ATTITUDES TO GROUP WORK: REPLICATION STUDIES

In retrospect the research design was too complicated, allowing too many choices and confounding the effects of curriculum topic and classroom organisation. The exercise was therefore repeated in local authority C but this time only six pictures were used. Given the fact that in the analysis of the comments in the previous exercise the teacher tended to dominate the exchanges whenever he or she was present, this time the focus was on the role of the teacher. The three pairs of pictures consisted of:

Pair 1   Teacher talking to an individual child versus teacher to the whole class.

Pair 2   A group of children discussing into a tape recorder with no teacher present versus the same activity with the teacher.

Pair 3   Children working on a practical task without the teacher and then with the teacher as displayed in Figure 3.4.

The schools in local authority C were 8–12 middle schools and cartoons were given to the first and fourth year pupils in the three schools taking part in the project involving a total of 372 children.

Once again, the results bore a similarity to those already described. Overall the children preferred working on the practical tasks (47 per cent) compared to receiving individual or class attention (41 per cent). By far the least popular activity was group discussion (12 per cent). Looking at the figures in Table 3.3 it can be seen that there is marginal preference for the group practical task rather than the situation where pupils were either receiving individual attention or were part of the class audience. Whole

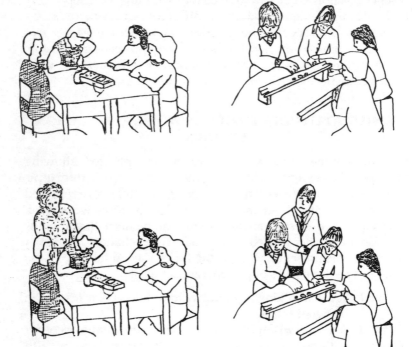

Figure 3.4 Pairs of cartoon pictures used in study of attitudes to group
work (teacher present versus teacher absent)

class teaching was marginally preferable to individual attention
(23 per cent against 18 per cent) while discussion with the teacher
(9 per cent) was to be preferred to discussion when the teacher
was not present. The reverse case was true of the practical task
where 26 per cent of the first preferences were given to the picture
where the teacher was not present compared to 21 per cent when
the teacher was part of the group.

Table 3.3 Pupils' first preferences of three pairs of cartoon pictures of the primary classroom, (expressed as per cent of 311 responses)

Pupil activity		*Teacher's role*			
		Teacher present	*Teacher absent*	*Class instruction*	*Total*
Pair A	Individual un-specified task	18	—	23	41
Pair B	Group discussion	9	3	—	12
Pair C	Group practical task	21	26	—	47
Total		48	29	23	100

In Table 3.3 the data comprise the responses of 311 pupils and not the 339 in the total sample. This is because of the unusual nature of the responses of one class of 12 year olds in one of the schools where a significantly different distribution of choices emerged during the extended analysis of choices by class and by age. Whereas only nine pupils from the remaining classes had chosen the discussion picture where the teacher was not present in this class, it was the first choice of nineteen of the pupils (nearly 68 per cent). When asked about the picture that they least liked only two pupils out of the twenty-eight in the class picked this picture. These two pupils complained that they did not like this way of working because it resulted in,

listening to one person
too many arguments.

On the other hand, the pupils who chose the picture offered many positive reasons for working together without the teacher,

It's good to work things out without the teacher.
You can discuss what you are doing.
You can find out what other people think.
You can have a laugh when you discuss.
You can help each other to discuss things.
You get the work done faster when everybody is listening.'

71

For this group teachers were seen as an irrelevance as several comments explained:

> I like to work with my friends and discuss things on our own because when you work with teachers they always stop you.
> I would rather do group work without the teacher because it gives you a chance to work with other people.
> One can learn more from each other when there is no teacher to nag.

Furthermore the reported conversations between pupils were very different in this class than in the others. Whereas for the remainder of the pupils the comments were very similar to those obtained from the study using twelve pictures where children generally exchanged information about whether their answers were correct or whether they had understood the teacher's instructions:

Pupil 1   It's number 1.
Pupil 2   No, it's number 5.

The comments of the children favouring group discussion tended to exhibit elements of abstract talk:

Pupil 1   I think the plague was caused by fleas.
Pupil 2   No, I think it was caused by rats.

This group's least favourite picture was being part of the class audience. They said of this situation:

> It's boring.
> Nobody's learning anything, only the teacher.
> You have to copy everything the teacher says.
> The teacher is telling you boring things about what happened long ago.
> It's boring sitting in silence, listening to a teacher.

With the other classes in all the pictures where the teacher was present the stress was again on teachers reprimanding pupils. In such cases the teachers' instructions were always brief and to the point.

> Get on with your work.
> Get writing.

Finish.
Now listen to me.
Stop it.
You'll not leave this room until you've finished.

As in the previous exercise many of these comments were associated with getting things wrong. This was closely associated with working on one's own which was usually associated with being behind. Here the teacher was saying,

Quite good but you've got this wrong.
I'll punish you. Do work on page 10–13 on maths.
I want you to carry on with your unfinished work because you are behind.

Some pupils complained that in this situation they couldn't be 'intermittent workers' as in the ORACLE I study.

With the teacher watching there's no one to play with.
There's no friends.

But there were, however, some who did enjoy individual working because,

I like working with the teacher on my own.
Discovering with the teacher is fun.

Once again it appeared that this emphasis on getting things right and being accused of not working if things were wrong produced considerable anxiety amongst many children. Dislike of working in groups was mainly because,

My friends made me silly.
There is no teacher.
I like writing at tables.
You're worried if you get things wrong.

and in these circumstances the children either sought to control each other's behaviour so that the group would not attract the teacher's attention or else gave reassurance to friends.

Shut up.
Get on.
Don't worry.
It will turn out allright.

Given the remarkable difference in attitude between the class of 12 year olds in one school and the remainder of the sample, it was decided to interview the pupils in their final year who had picked discussing in groups without the teacher as their first choice. Some of this interview, which lasted for one and a half hours, has already been reported in Galton (1989). It was these pupils, quoted in the first chapter, who continued to work in groups against the instructions of their present teacher, by discussing ideas when they were at home over the telephone. During the interview the tape had to be turned off at certain points because the children wished to talk forcibly about situations where they felt either upset or frightened during lessons and named particular teachers. Even so, they agreed, at the end of the discussion that the tapes should be played back to the staff in the school. Strong feelings emerged about ownership of work and particularly about teachers joining groups and imposing their own ideas. Evidence of fear of failure was very strong, with one pupil describing question and answer sessions during a class discussion as 'like walking on a tightrope'. They also complained about not understanding why they were doing things. Because, as one pupil argued,

If I could see what it was learning me I could do it but I don't see what it is learning me.

They also explained the various strategies they adopted for dealing with work which they either didn't understand or which they found repetitive and boring. When told to write a four page essay, 'You put big gaps in your words . . . and get bigger writing . . . use bigger words like "investigation"'. All sorts of strategies existed for avoiding answering questions such as always putting your hand up (obviously less effective in a small group than with a whole class where there was a 1 in 30 chance of being picked) then hesitating before giving an answer. When the teacher supplied the correct answer the pupil would then say, 'Oh yes, that's it', pretending that the correct answer had been 'on the tip of your tongue'.

Repeatedly, however, the discussion came back to an uncertainty that existed in the pupils' minds about how their ideas would be received by the teacher. These pupils said that they had no way of knowing when a teacher was going to respond positively to what they were doing in the groups,

You never know when they are going to shout at you. Sometimes you could be saying something and they like agree with you. But like next minute they can just turn against you and shout at you for something like that.

This explained why teachers found it difficult to come to the group and just sit and watch because, according to the pupils, when this happens,

You get nervous when someone is around. You feel uncomfortable like when they're there. If you do anything wrong you think, Oh no!

As the interview progressed the issues crystallised around the different functions of the teacher as someone who listened to your ideas but, at the same time, had to check up to see that you were working. Although the majority of pupils thought that the teacher should offer help only,

When you ask for it. They shouldn't say anything until we ask them. They should sit quiet.

Some said this was a problem because

The teacher comes up to you then like you go all shy. That's when you really need some help because you don't know what to do. But when you do know what to do properly you get stuck in and you ignore the teacher.

However, the recurring theme concerned the uncertainty about the teacher's role.

If you were in a group and you were all writing about different things for about half an hour, she comes up and says, 'How much have you done?' and you say, 'Not much.' and you get done and we are discussing it really.

It was at this point that they asked,

Can we mention a certain teacher?

and the tape was turned off. Not all teachers, however, were the subject of these criticisms. When the tape was switched on once more the interviewer asked,

Interviewer: What about teachers who give you confidence?
Chorus of pupils: Yes, Yes. Mrs Wright's like that.

Girl pupil: She sits down at the end. She says, 'Do you mind me saying anything?' She's right down to earth like. She'll come and listen. She'll listen to you. . . . says you'll learn by your mistakes so . . . she doesn't go all irate. She tells you your mistakes that you have done and then she just tells you to put them right and then she comes back in a bit. She knows what work you want to do and that.

As the discussion progressed it seemed clear that Mrs Wright's role had been a crucial one in helping these children to develop positive attitudes towards group work, attitudes which were reflected in their practice and which had been continued even after she had ceased to be their teacher. Accordingly, it was decided that the research would progressively focus on this teacher's practice in an effort to identify some of the key strategies which helped foster collaboration among pupils in this particular classroom. It is to this third phase of the research that we now turn in the following chapter.

4

A TALE OF TWO TEACHERS
Initial encounters

WORKING IN GROUPS: PUPILS' PERCEPTIONS

Before describing the next stage of the research it would seem useful to attempt a summary of the main issues which emerge from the previous chapter. First, from the pupils' point of view, there is considerable uncertainty and indecision when working in groups. Part of this uncertainty comes from pupils not knowing why they are doing things so that, at least in the early stages, until they have 'sussed it out' they are reluctant to participate. However, once a group is well established it develops a strong sense of solidarity. In such a group you feel able to 'face up to the teacher' whereas 'on your own you have no chance'.

Second, in the comments of the pupils during the interviews and in the phrases they attribute to the teacher in the cartoons, there is an overwhelming emphasis on negative aspects of behaviour. In the cartoon pictures, teachers are portrayed as highly critical, particularly when the pupil has made a mistake in his or her work or obtained an incorrect result. According to the children the teacher often attributes the cause of the pupil's failure to either lack of concentration or to disruptive behaviour. In the cartoon responses, pupils are accused of 'not paying attention', 'fooling around' or 'not getting on' quickly enough. Rarely do the children write statements where the teacher says, 'let's see if I can help you with this problem'. This makes some pupils (and we might assume that these are the least confident ones) feel 'nervous' and 'shy' when the teacher comes to the group.

Third, certain pupils, perhaps the more confident ones, express strong feelings about retaining the ownership of their ideas. They complain that teachers would sometimes come and

77

change their work and when that happened 'it didn't feel so good'. They complained too of inconsistencies in some teachers' behaviour, quoting one example where having become so engrossed in a discussion about the issues that they had not completed the written assignment, they had been told off as a result. The teacher had accused them of chatting and wasting time. This kind of incident reinforces the pupils' uncertainty about the purpose of group work because when they engage successfully in collaboration, which they see as the aim of working together in a group, they are then criticised for not completing their individual assignments.

Finally, most pupils expressed a strong dislike of discussion and a preference for practical tasks. In the light of the previous paragraphs it would seem that the latter activities presented fewer problems since both the purposes of collaboration and the desired outcome were far clearer than in a situation where pupils discussed ideas with no clear understanding of whether or not they would be acceptable to the teacher.

WORKING IN GROUPS: TEACHERS' REACTIONS

In the last chapter we saw that many of the children's comments of what pupils were saying to each other in the cartoon pictures reflected very closely the kinds of conversations which were typically recorded by observers in both the ORACLE and the PRISMS study. As a result these findings present considerable problems for teachers, particularly because in Arnold's (1962) terms the attitudes expressed appear not only evaluative but also motivational and therefore lead to action (or in some cases inaction). The ORACLE research, particularly the study dealing with transfer (Galton and Willcocks 1983) contains numerous examples of strategies of avoidance that pupils employed in order to escape expressing their ideas to the teacher and these were also described during the interview reported in the previous chapter. Other pupils appeared to abandon the attempt to express ideas and instead preferred the teacher to direct all aspects of their life in the classroom.

From the point of view of a teacher, whose goal is to develop co-operative attitudes among the pupils, the world of the classroom portrayed by these children presents some formidable challenges and poses a series of teaching dilemmas. Indeed it readily becomes apparent why classroom observational research has repeatedly come up with the finding that there is little collaboration among pupils in the primary classroom and that teachers, as a whole, although they approve and support the aims of group work, show a marked reluctance to use it as a major teaching strategy. There will also be some teachers, having read the previous pages, who will feel concern at what has been presented, seeing it as yet another attack on their efforts at a time when the profession, as a whole, feels undervalued. This was certainly the feeling of some of the staff in the school where the interview with the pupils quoted earlier took place. This feeling was partly exacerbated because at the end of the interview the pupils came out and told some teachers, 'we really told him (the interviewer) what it is like here'. The headteacher felt that the tape should be edited in order to remove names of teachers. As a result there was an interval before staff could hear what children had said and this increased their degree of apprehension.

When the tape was finally played these anxieties were, to some extent, relieved in that the interviewer could regularly be heard putting the teachers' view of the situation to the pupils, rather than simply encouraging them to 'sound off'. Listening to the tape, however, was for many of the teachers a painful experience. For some, the explanation for what the pupils said could be found in the dominant role taken by one or two pupils about whom it was remarked they were 'typical barrack room lawyers'. Unlike the interviewer these teachers had not been present to see the faces of other children and the nods of agreement when, for example, one pupil had described answering a teacher's question as 'walking on a tightrope'. There was a tendency for the teachers to ignore the points on the tape where the interviewer stopped and asked the class whether they agreed with what someone had said to ensure the spokesperson was speaking for others as well as him or herself. All staff were affected by the experience. Those teachers who acknowledged the full significance of these confirmatory interventions felt very demoralised by the experience. Some felt like giving up teaching, expressing the view that they had been wasting their time all these years. What hurt them most was the thought that the teacher–pupil relationship, which the school had tried hard to develop and of which they were justly proud, was not always at it appeared to be.

It needs to be stressed, therefore, that these teachers were all highly dedicated and that the school enjoyed an excellent reputation among parents and among other teachers in the local authority. All the teachers, that is until the introduction of the teachers' contract, (setting out terms of employment, including the number of hours to be spent in school) worked extraordinarily long hours and would go to almost any lengths to help a child with a problem. They, of course, did not see themselves as being in any way different from colleagues in other schools. Like all of us at times they found themselves, when teaching, under great stress and behaved in ways which, in retrospect, they would have preferred not to have done. What, however, had emerged from the attitude measures and from the subsequent interview was that these infrequent incidents seemed to loom large in the minds of the pupils and to colour their judgements about all aspects of their school activity in very significant ways. The account which follows, therefore, although necessarily personalised, should not be treated complacently as an appraisal of another teacher's performance. The difficulties which are described do not arise because of the weaknesses of a particular teacher but are part of the general problem of attempting to encourage group work. With the exception of a minority of extremely gifted human beings, such difficulties can be discovered in most classrooms. To emphasise this point it is perhaps pertinent to say something about the background of the school and the staff and their involvement in the research programme, before going on to discuss the findings of this next phase of the research.

THE SCHOOLS AND TEACHERS IN PHASE THREE OF THE PROJECT

In its original form, ORACLE II (Effective Group Work in the Primary Classroom) involved the same three authorities where the observations had been carried out during the ORACLE I project. However, in the early stage, the failure to identify a sufficient number of 'expert' teachers who could induct their colleagues into the art of working collaboratively made it necessary for the research team to act as consultants in an additional action research phase of the study. As a result the small research team became overstretched and could no longer support similar programmes in each of the three local authorities. Work in local authority A was reduced with teachers acting as evaluators for some of the strategies being developed by the teachers from local authority B where the main thrust of the programme was centred. There was, however, a special working relationship with three schools in local authority C and, because of this, it was decided to continue the collaboration between these teachers and the project team.

One attractive feature of this relationship was the close understanding between the headteachers and the Director of the research team, an understanding which had developed during the lifetime of the first ORACLE project. In that study one school, let us call it Corefield, had done exceptionally well on some of the indicators associated with teacher effectiveness. Two of the teachers observed subsequently proved to be 'infrequent changers', a type of teacher who was characterised by frequent use of high-level cognitive questioning, low levels of pupil distraction and better than average levels of task-related feedback. Their pupils enjoyed considerable success both on measures of basic skills and on what were termed study skills involving listening with understanding and communicating clearly in speech. At the end of the first ORACLE study the headteacher of Corefield left to take up a post as adviser in the neighbouring authority and the deputy headteacher, Martin Cox, left to take up a headship at Burwood Middle (8–12) school. Burwood was an old school but it was to move into a new open plan building at the end of that year. Another teacher from Corefield, John Thompson, a key member of staff, had left in the previous year to take up an appointment as deputy head, having been observed during two of the three years of fieldwork in ORACLE I. Thus by the end of the first phase of ORACLE, Corefield had lost three senior members of staff in rapid succession although it retained the services of two other teachers who had also been observed during Stage I of the ORACLE project.

By the time the first year of ORACLE II had ended and the decision taken to engage in an action research programme with groups of volunteered teachers, a further change had taken place. Martin Cox had by now moved into his new open-plan school and John Thompson, who had moved to a deputy headship, was promoted to a headteacher after only two years. He took over a school which was adjacent to the new school at Burwood, a school we shall call Whitegates. Thus a very close relationship existed between certain teachers in these three schools and the ORACLE research team.

At the time, one of the issues under discussion among action researchers concerned the effectiveness of networking between schools. The replacement of the Schools Council by the Schools Curriculum Development Committee (SCDC) had led to increased interest in school-based curriculum development, which was in part a reaction to the lack of success of larger centre to periphery projects. Action research was seen, by many, as an ideal way of facilitating this form of curriculum change but one drawback was the number of consultants needed to enable this localised approach to be used on a relatively large scale. The solution of developing networks of self-supporting schools was put forward as a means of overcoming some of these difficulties. The three schools, Burwood, Corefield and Whitegates, with their close association, offered an ideal situation in which to try out this networking principle.

Events, however, conspired against this plan. Although the association of the three schools continued over two years and culminated in an in-service day for all other middle schools in local authority C, both Corefield and Whitegates gradually withdrew from the project leaving the bulk of the work to continue at Burwood. One of the main features of Corefield over this period was a rapid change in deputy heads, three of whom were appointed and then promoted within the two years of the project. Added to this one teacher, the most successful from the first ORACLE project, transferred to Burwood, and Corefield's headteacher was absent for a considerable period due to illness. For different reasons Whitegates also withdrew. In the second year of the project the school underwent a total 'face lift' and the headteacher, John Thompson, felt that the pressures that staff were under during this period were such that they could no longer make a useful contribution.

ORACLE II, therefore, officially ended in 1983 without any real progress having been made towards the solution of some of the problems outlined in the previous chapter. At Burwood, the results of the cartoon exercise, and the comments of the pupils during the subsequent interview, made the headteacher, Martin Cox, aware that some benefit might arise if teachers, whom the pupils had said gave them confidence when working in groups, were teamed with others about whom the same pupils had expressed reservations. Of particular interest was the pairing of Jean Wright, whom the children had specifically mentioned, with

Norma Reynolds in the Year 2 (9+) base. These two teachers shared a large open-plan area with the Year 1 (8+) base who were taught by Jane Thompson and Sylvia Wells. Jean Wright was the co-ordinator in charge of this team.

The academic year 1984/85 also coincided with the implementation of the new CATE (Council for Accreditation of Teacher Education) regulations whereby those training teachers were required to gain recent and relevant successful experience in the classroom. This provided the stimulus for one of the authors to take up residence in local authority C for a six-week period and to work alongside the two teachers, Norma and Jean, with a view to identifying some of the particular practices which gave rise to the comments of the pupils during the interview.

Subsequently, when it became known that a professor was returning to the classroom, albeit for a short period, interest was expressed by the educational media and led to an agreement to make a film for the Open University as part of a new Master's degree course on classroom research. The film was recorded in the following year (1986) when the children were in Year 3 (10+ year) and the two teachers, Norma and Jean, arranged to take over these classes for a short period, prior to the filming. It was agreed between the two that they would develop work around a common theme, 'Movement', and that filming would consist of two lessons, one in creative arts and the other in science. For both lessons the two parallel classes would use exactly the same materials and the tasks set would be the same. In the first lesson the children were to observe a group of pupils moving to music and then be asked to express this movement pictorially, with each group deciding on an appropriate medium. In the science lesson the task was to make a timing device which could record movement for exactly two minutes. The children were given a range of materials such as water, sand, empty plastic containers, candles and string and had, as a group, to decide on an appropriate method for constructing a timer. After each lesson the teachers were interviewed and asked to comment on what had taken place. The presence of an Open University BBC Film Unit guaranteed that the product would be of high quality. Full transcripts were available for all four lessons and the film itself had superimposed upon it a digital clock so that frequencies of interactions and pauses could be calculated to the nearest second.

THE SECOND GROUP WORK EXPERIMENT

The circumstances described in the previous section constituted possibly a unique opportunity to conduct an educational experiment with control of the major factors other than the teaching style. In the previous year the two teachers, Norma and Jean, had been randomly assigned to the two classes which were, as far as possible, comparable in terms of mixed ability. In the filmed teaching episodes both the content of the lessons and the environment were the same, since in the latter case, the pupils from each class replaced each other in the same base area where the cameras had been set up. In this particular study, no attempt was made to assess the quality of the products since only one particular lesson was observed and the subsequent conditions, when further lessons took place, could not be controlled in the same way.

Analysis of the video tapes of the four lessons showed the following:

1 In both of Norma's lessons the children, typically, elected to produce individual products while in Jean's class they agreed upon a joint outcome. This resulted in higher levels of pupil–pupil discussion. In the sequences recorded (although it must be remembered that the camera was selective in its focus) there were far more pupil–pupil extended exchanges lasting beyond a 25 second interval in Jean's class. In all approximately 49 per cent of pupil–pupil interaction within Jean's lessons consisted of sustained conversation compared to just under 20 per cent in Norma's. Caution needs to be employed when interpreting this finding, because of the different teaching approaches used by Norma and Jean. In Norma's case the camera tended to focus less frequently on pupils following her as she moved from table to table.

2 Not only the level but also the content of discussions between pupils differed. Whereas in Norma's class the exchanges between pupils mainly concerned practical matters involving the mechanical activities connected with the task, the pupils in Jean's class tended to engage in more challenging conversations. The distinction made by Bennett and Dunne (1989) between instrumental talk and abstract talk could be applied to these exchanges.

Thus in Norma's class the following conversation occurred between two pupils:

Pupil 1 Shall I put some more water?
Pupil 2 No, just leave it. Take it off again.
Pupil 1 Are you ready to start again?
Pupil 2 No. Take it off. Ready. Are you ready? Put it on. Ready. Go.
Pupil 3 One minute.
Pupil 1 Just get on with that idea you are thinking about. That other idea. (to Pupil 2)
Pupil 2 Allright.

Here, in this extract, Pupil 2 acts as leader and enlists two other pupils in the group to help him pour water through a funnel. Pupil 1 fills up the water reservoir while Pupil 3 uses a stopwatch to time the flow of water through the funnel. At the end of the sequence Pupil 1 tells Pupil 2 to get on with her own experiment.

In contrast to this exchange there is evidence of more abstract discussion in the following extract recorded during Jean's lesson on the same topic (making a two-minute timer):

Pupil 1 What can we do now then?
Pupil 2 Well, how else could we have the strength? We could double it on top.
Pupil 3 What would that do? We have got the string going from this side to that side. You don't want the string going like this because it will snap. Here get the string vertical somehow. That would work.
Pupil 1 Why do we need to tie it on to the bottle then? Wouldn't it be better to tie it on to something else? If we are going to put it vertical it wouldn't help to tie it on the bottle . . . get it on fire and hold it up.
Pupil 2 Do we actually need the candle if we are going to burn the string?
Pupil 1 No. Because you just have to light it.
Pupil 2 Yeah. Anyway . . . let's light it and hold it up to see if it goes up.

In this extract the group of pupils are attempting to suspend a length of string and to burn it, rather like a fuse. Initially, the

85

string is tied to the tops of two plastic lemonade bottles which are half filled with water to act as weights. The string is suspended horizontally across two supports, the bottles acting as a source of tension to keep the string taut. A metre rule is placed next to the string to measure the distance over which the string burns during two minutes. The recorded extract shows that before trying out this experiment the children foresee weaknesses in the design, namely that once the string is lit, the tension due to the weighted bottles will cause it to snap. They, therefore, examine the possibility of suspending the string vertically, measuring the length of string burnt as the flame moves from bottom to the top of the vertical plane. Not only is there evidence of abstract reasoning within the recorded sequence but also it is clear that the pupils are more receptive to each other's comments and ideas in contrast to the extract recorded in Norma's class.

Thus, in terms of the definitions offered in Chapter 1 (p. 10) Jean's pupils appear to be involved in collaborative activity engaging co-operatively on a task with a joint outcome in mind. In Norma's class the level of group activity remains at the co-operative stage in which the pupils, although working on a common task, nevertheless prefer to produce individual responses rather than a joint outcome. The filmed episode supports the evidence of the cartoon pictures where in Jean Wright's class, the children tended to report abstract conversations, whereas with other teachers' classes the pupils described shorter conversations to do with practical matters.

The following attempt to explain these differences is based on both further analysis of these filmed episodes and also on the reflections of the author during the period when he taught alongside Norma and Jean. As such, the style is different from previous chapters, since the fieldnotes recorded during my period of 'recent and relevant' experience were written in the first person and for the sake of accuracy have been left unaltered. Although a number of issues was raised during this teaching experience and has been commented on elsewhere (Galton 1989) the analysis here concerns the three specific areas where pupils, during the subsequent interview, following the cartoon exercise, expressed concern.

The first deals with the problem of 'not knowing what it was learning us'. In particular the analysis examines the way in which the two teachers explained to pupils what they were required to do. The second issue concerns the accusation by pupils that teachers interfered with their ideas by coming to the group and 'taking over'. Here the manner in which the two teachers interacted with the pupils once the lesson commenced is the major focus. Finally, the third part of the analysis examines the question of behaviour and the way in which both teachers maintained classroom control. In both the cartoon pictures and in the subsequent interview pupils expressed very strong feelings about their uncertainty over what teachers would do or say when they came to a group. On some occasions, for example, they claimed teachers would praise ideas whereas on other occasions the pupil would be 'told off'.

DEFINING TASKS: TELLING PUPILS WHAT TO DO AND HOW TO DO IT

The analysis presented in this section seeks to establish the following propositions.

Proposition 1

When providing instructions, for example at the beginning of a teaching session, the task is usually defined in terms of an end product. Children are told what they have to do in order to complete their assignment satisfactorily. Often this advice is coupled with routine instructions about the resources needed and their availability and location and sometimes these instructions are also associated with rules concerning behaviour while carrying out the task. *Rarely do the instructions offer reasons why the pupil is doing the particular task.*

Thus in local authority B (where it will be remembered teachers taking part in the first group experiment were required to make a tape recording of their initial introduction to the topic) in none of the twenty recorded introductions, did a teacher do other than explain what the children had to do in order to complete the assignment. In over two-thirds of these introductions children were also told how they should behave while completing the task. Thus they should be 'sensible' or, in cases where they were going out of the school to conduct the activity, they should remember that 'they represented the school'. In none of the twenty cases was it explained to children how they should co-operate while in the group or what procedures they should adopt when problems occurred such as disagreements. Children were simply directed to work in their groups without further explanation.

Proposition 2

One major consequence of introducing topics in this way is that the children concentrate on completing the task as soon as possible. Often in these cases the group will renegotiate the task in order to eliminate those elements within it which are designed to improve the quality of the solutions but slow down completion. Hence the finding, reported in a previous chapter, that when set an open-ended problem with several possible solutions the children accept the first one suggested. For example, in science experiments, where data must be collected under carefully controlled conditions, the conditions will be ignored so that pupils engage in such tasks with what my diary fieldnotes term 'an undisciplined approach'.

Proposition 3

This 'undisciplined approach' creates a cycle of frustration, whereby teachers spend much of the lesson repeating the instructions in an effort to slow down the children's progress towards a too rapid solution of the problem. The children, in turn, resent the fact that the teacher is interfering and stopping them from working. This cycle can only be broken, as will be illustrated in Jean's case, if more time is spent during introductions emphasising the importance of the processes to be used during the task.

In the diary fieldnotes there are constant references to the problem of pupils adopting an 'undisciplined' approach to task activities. This is particularly true of a science project where both Norma's and Jean's classes were engaged in topics related to the local environment. Norma's class was investigating the local wood, studying the creatures in it, the composition of the soil and the kinds of plants and leaves to be found within this environment. Jean's class was involved in similar activities but these were located in and around a nearby stream.

Before describing several incidents during this environmental topic a more straightforward illustration of the first two propositions can be found in the fieldnotes for the first day of my time at Burwood.

For the second period until lunchtime I helped with number work. The children start with a worksheet containing simple revisions and are then to go on to various games which are designed to reinforce the skills that they have been using. There are three groups, one doing factors and multiplication, one take aways and the other place value. The children working on factors still have problems with multiplication and continually come to ask whether four goes into forty-eight or thirty-six etc.

When we get to the games I am faced with a dilemma. The group who were doing factors are now playing a numerical form of snakes and ladders. The children throw a dice and move a counter along the required number of places on a board marked from 1 to 100. If the counter lands on a 5 or a multiple of 5 then they move forward a further 5 positions. Thus, for example, if the counter lands on 15 they will move to 20. If, however, the counter lands on 7 or a multiple of 7 they have to move back 7 places so that, for example, if the counter lands on 28 they then move back to 21. Landing on 35 or 70 allows you to move back only 2 places since you move forward 5 and then back 7.

I watch the children play and it is clear that they are only interested in getting to 100 as fast as possible. In some cases they do move up 5 but never back 7. They rearrange the game so that you throw a dice and always move the counter forward the number of places which appear on the upward face of the dice. I try to explain the game to them again but it is clear that they can't recognise the multiples of 7 so that when a counter lands on one of these squares nobody challenges the pupil to move back. I sit with them for a little while and when the next person lands on a multiple of 7 I stop the game and try to work out with them whether the rule needs to be applied.

But I see boredom (and slight hostility) in their faces. Who is this person spoiling their game? Why can't they just move the counters on as they want and win? From a teacher's point of view, however, there doesn't seem much point in playing the game unless the children are doing more than counting. My being there does make them focus on the 7 times table, the point of the game, but it is very counterproductive in terms of their motivation and their interest.

Afterwards I discuss what happened with the other base teachers. Interestingly, no one comes up with the suggestion that we should explain to the children the purpose of the game but earlier when I asked the pupils who were playing 5s and 7s why they were playing the game they didn't know and replied 'It's just a game'.

(Fieldnote diary 22 April)

In this extract we see pupils renegotiating the task to speed up the process whereby they can complete the game. Playing the game according to the rules would have taken them considerably longer, not only because, in some cases, they would have had to move back seven squares but also because of the time it would take to work through the seven times table in every case. Not surprisingly, because no one explained that the purpose of the game was to spend this additional time practising the seven and five times table, the pupils dispensed with this part of the proce- dure and contented themselves with moving the counter the number of places shown on the upturned face of the dice. In this way they completed the game as quickly as possible.

Similar behaviour manifested itself on the first occasion when Norma's class paid a visit to the woods to collect soil samples. On the day before the visit Norma spent some time showing pupils how to construct a metre square using four pegs and string. The children practised this task in the play area around the school. Using the metre square ensured that each group of pupils collected soil and debris from the same-sized area. They could then examine, fairly, how these samples, collected from different locations, differed. However, as the diary records, the first visit to the woods did not go according to plan.

We get to the woods. Norma tells the children to go and find a reasonable place to set up their string grid and then to draw and map out what they see and to investigate the contents of each square and record it. The children wander off. In their enthusiasm and excitement they begin to use their forks to dig at the soil and collect specimens. Most of the children quickly abandon the idea of making the grid in favour of exploring what lies under the ground so that I construct a grid for them and this they are happy to let me do. By now all the other groups know that if they hadn't got the grid I will come along and help them do it. But time passes quickly and if the grids are not done soon there will not be time to collect the samples. Eventually with a lot of help everyone has collected something and we have remembered to put a piece of paper in each of the sample bags indicating which part of the grid we collected leaves or soils or insects.

We get back to school with only a few minutes left before the end of the day and there is just time to finish off the labelling of the specimens and to promise the children we will look at them first thing tomorrow. Norma is very good at opening up the discussion of what we learnt and how a trip like this can be better organised on another occasion. I like the way she takes the blame for some of the difficulties we had.

(Fieldnote diary 30 April)

Talking over matters afterwards it is easy to conclude that, on this first occasion, the children should have been left to explore the environment leaving more systematic work until later but, as Norma pointed out, there were constraints of time. What is not discussed, however, is her introduction which mainly concentrated on ways of collecting the soil and the need to label the specimens. While both factors were important, at no time was any explanation given as to why these soil samples should be sampled from within different parts of the metre grid. Not surprisingly the children ignored this part of the instructions in favour of collecting as many soil samples as possible.

However, the fieldnote was written from the standpoint of an observer looking at Norma's approach. It is a different story when, as the participant observer, I attempt to evaluate my own performance. Now the constraints and problems which faced Norma in the earlier episode are more vividly portrayed.

This morning I am to take one of the groups off to their second visit to the woods. I am using the jig-saw grouping arrangement so that each member of the party belongs to

91

another group in the class who are investigating different soil topics. Each pupil has their own list of tasks to complete. Some are collecting samples of leaves at different distances from a tree, others are looking for plants. We decide to take a camera in order to photograph the sites that we are studying so that the pictures can form a part of our display.

We recall the things we need to take and the children go off and get these quietly. On the way to the woods there is a certain amount of giggling and fooling. Lisa tucks her arm in mine and clearly thinks it's grand to have 'a friend'. The children are very skilful at manipulating me. They quickly extract a promise to go to the swings (next to the wood) if they work well. We arrive at the wood, however, and immediately all their good intentions seem to vanish. In their enthusiasm the children rush around hither and thither looking at things and I am very reluctant to bring them back to the point where we try to study the area more systematically. Then my first mistake of the morning is exposed. I forgot to tell them to go to the lavatory before we started. Ruth is now hopping up and down desperately demanding to go to the toilet which, of course, is conveniently near the swings. Since I can't let one little girl go off by herself we beat a strategic retreat and I decided to have an early break so that we can have our play. We collect our samples and go off.

After break we begin again. The children sit on two benches and write up what they have found. I don't really want them to write anything until we have discussed things but they are desperate to get something down on paper. As we walk back through the woods we collect samples of fungi and twigs for further examination. But the children seem to have become obsessed with the idea of labelling. Perhaps because I have stressed too much the need to make certain that one knows what is in the bag. It seems to come almost as a relief for them to have something clear cut by way of a demand so that for them the test of success seems to be the number of labelled specimens they can collect and the resolutions that we took together at the beginning of the morning to carry out specific activities in a more systematic way have been abandoned. On the other hand if I tried to

92

raise the issue with them such as fair testing or accurate recording I immediately begin to see the changed expression on their faces, ranging from Lisa's panic, 'OK and tell us what you want us to do' to Ian's resentment, 'I am enjoying myself. Why are you trying to stop me doing what I am enjoying?'

(Fieldnote diary 3 May)

As teachers we have all experienced occasions when, perhaps unthinkingly, we stress the outcomes of the investigation rather than the importance of the processes. This comes about largely from the pressure to produce something worthwhile in a limited amount of time available, something that the children can be praised for and which they can show off to parents. These problems of time are often exacerbated because of the numerous unplanned events which impede progress towards a satisfactory outcome. At Burwood, for example, plans often had to be modified at the last moment because of 'trade offs' with other teachers for the use of suitable rooms.

Even accepting that a more skilful practitioner than I might have managed the situation more effectively there still remains a sense of dissatisfaction when placing these accounts against those of Michael Armstrong's (1981) and Stephen Rowland's (1987) descriptions of children who gradually move from a position of undisciplined enthusiasm to systematic inquiry. While acknowledging the strength of Rowland's claim that children reconstruct existing frameworks of knowledge only when they have 'ownership' of their work (so that direct instruction by the teacher should take place only when the pupil perceives the need for such instruction), such an approach does seem an inadequate response to the pressures reflected in the above accounts which would, from observation, appear to be typical of many classrooms. In Rowland's (1987) account of the pupil Dean who 'confronted problems of classification and taxonomy in great depth' direct instruction was given in the use of fractions at the point when Dean came to appreciate that he needed this help in order to continue with his investigation. However, in the classroom at Burwood, not all the children seemed like Dean and they appeared to prefer changing the nature of the task, as in the number game, to avoid having to expose their inability to recognise multiples of seven. In Rowland's approach the pupil is left to appreciate that how a task is tackled is just as important as how it looks when completed. But the reality of classroom life, as daily faced by many teachers and pupils, suggests that such an approach can be problematic and very time consuming.

One alternative is to break down the processes involved into smaller units and to devise structured exercises to illustrate the value of each component, so that children come to understand that the process is as important as the outcome. This was the approach adopted by Jean who, at the beginning of the year when introducing group work to the children, stressed that one of its purposes was to share ideas in seeking the best solution to a problem. Pupils were asked to play a game which would demonstrate the truth of this statement. They were given a sheet in which they had to tick from a survival list, six items of equipment they would keep from an aircraft that had just crashed in the desert. The actual exercise was based on one used by the RAF. Having completed the task children were then told to get into pairs to compare answers. It became clear that many pupils completed the checklist by making different assumptions about the correct procedure to employ while awaiting rescue. Some children assumed that the best plan was to stay by the aircraft and wait to be rescued. They therefore chose to retain the overcoat because the information provided told them that the temperature dropped at night. Those, however, who had decided that the best solution was to walk across the desert to the neighbouring oasis in search of water, naturally discarded the overcoat but retained the compass. At the end of the task Jean made the point to the children, very strongly, that if this had been a real live situation, being able to share ideas might have saved lives since, until the two alternative solutions were compared, most children had not thought there was any other way of solving the problem but the one they had originally selected. In further sessions children went on to consider some of the skills necessary to listen to each other's ideas.

As the year progressed, however, there appeared an assumption, on Jean's part, that there was little need to reinforce this initial exposition. Gradually more emphasis was placed upon the outcomes and on the organisation of the task and less importance was placed upon the group processes themselves. Thus, in the case of the mathematics game, Jean did not explain to the children that the purpose was to practise a set of skills that the previous mathematics exercise had shown were lacking. It would seem important, therefore, for teachers continually to reinforce the skills involved in the group process if children are to feel confident enough to express and debate their ideas.

It is of interest, therefore, to see that when meeting the children again after the lapse of two terms Jean again reverts to the strategies used at the beginning of the previous school year and in her introduction to the 'timer' lesson stresses the group process. She tells the children,

> We have talked about fair testing before in our experiments. For this it is no good doing a one off and saying it's finished. You've got to test it and see if your device is accurate. Is it as accurate as it was the first time? Was the first result a freak? So test it. If you get finished within this lesson, I mean some of you might do it really quickly, others might never get anything ready that is going to work and will work for two minutes. Remember it's not getting it done that's really the important thing. It's not making a device that's the important thing. It's the talking and working together and planning it out and testing your apparatus. That's the really important thing and trying things out and getting your ideas across. OK? Don't just do things and then ignore the others.

In contrast Norma's introduction to the same lesson concentrates more strongly on making the device rather than on the way in which the children should work together. Norma begins by asking the class why it is important to measure time and when a pupil replies 'So that you can plan out what you are going to do', she continues,

> When I was thinking about this I thought two minutes is a nice time. You have got a tray of resources here. You have got plastic bottles, candles, lots of things in there. You don't have to use them all, select the ones that you think might work best to create your timer. Each group has the same tray of resources. Over there is a communal area where we have got extra bottles, coloured water, more plasticine, rubber bands, funnels, sugar. One thing can I just ask you. Don't ask me if this is right and don't ask me what I think because in my head I have got a real idea of how I would make the timer and what I don't want to do is tell you how

95

to do it. I want you to think of it. Create it yourselves. You will be working in your groups of twos and threes. Don't dive in and get cracking straight away. Discuss it at length and see what you have got in your tray and then start to apply the task.

Here, although there is a reference to working in groups, no explanation is given of why this is important and the focus is on the nature of the resources available for completing the task. There is an interesting editorial feature on the film in that, while Norma is talking to the children about the importance of time, the camera moves slowly along the row of pupils who are seated on the carpet in front of her. In so doing it picks out the fact that almost every child has a cheap digital wrist watch. One cannot help but speculate that perhaps some of these pupils might be asking;

If time is so important then why are we trying to measure it with bits of string and lighted candles rather than with a watch?

Of course, the real purpose of the exercise was not to measure time but to encourage children to work together co-operatively in order to solve a problem. Making the timing device was chosen because it was a very convenient and simple exercise but no one told these particular children this fact and so, not surprisingly, they tended to focus on completing the task rather than on discussing the best way to do it.

This emphasis upon the outcomes and the focus which pupils then place upon task completion creates a style of teacher–pupil interaction, where corrective or (evaluative) feedback predominates. The teacher is continually having to remind children of improved ways of carrying out the task, leading to the conclusion, by the pupils, that 'she wants to put her ideas because she thinks they're best'. Creating an ethos where critical feedback occurs (Rowland 1987) can be difficult. During such feedback 'students and teacher are engaged in a two way process of expressing what it is they are trying to formulate and grasping those things which the other person is indicating' (Rowland 1987: 131). The initial period, after the pupils have received their instructions and commenced the task, appears critical. It is to the study of Norma's and Jean's behaviour, in this respect, to which we now turn in the next chapter.

5

A TALE OF TWO TEACHERS
Facilitating collaboration

MAINTAINING GROUP ACTIVITY

In this chapter we continue the analysis of Norma's and Jean's teaching styles. The responses to the cartoon pictures described in Chapter 3 showed that the pupils made continual reference to receiving corrective (evaluative) feedback. There were repeated instances of exchanging information to find out if a sum was right or if a word had been spelt correctly. The incidents, described in my diary, reflected the views of other researchers that getting things right (or in many cases, not being found out doing something wrong) becomes a major preoccupation in the daily life of pupils in our schools. As described by John Holt (1984), for example, this fear of failure leads children to become 'fence stragglers' while Measor and Woods (1984) refer to similar strategies as 'knife edging'. One favoured technique used by pupils is to draw the teacher into the discussion whereby he or she provides more and more clues about what is an acceptable answer.

The study of this teacher dependency became a major focus of the diary. As a result of watching the children play the number game (described in the previous chapter) it was decided to develop a computer task that the children could do by themselves which would, as far as possible, be user friendly. This game was designed to be interactive so that the child could enter his or her name and have the computer address them personally. Pupils also had a measure of control over the process. They could decide the numbers from two to ten they wished to select and could also get help when in difficulties. The purpose of the game was explained, for example, they would improve their knowledge of

97

multiples of seven. For each turn the computer selected a random number, equivalent to the throw of the dice. The pupils were required to say how many spaces they needed to move forward and if the answer was correct the number of moves was recorded until they won the game by amassing a total of 100. Pupils helped to improve the game by giving their opinions at the design stage. Even so, for some children, playing this game proved a stressful activity. My fieldnotes record:

> The programme goes quite well. Anthony who played the game during the first week using the board is pleased when the machine remembers his name and sends him messages. He quickly gets the idea of checking his answer against the one in the computer but still doesn't remember his seven times table. However, he develops his own strategy which enables him to check the answer although it is a very long winded one. What he does is to count in sevens beginning at one each time. I wait to see if he will get the idea that he only has to count on from the last seven and not go right back to the beginning but he doesn't. The next group of children appear more confident mathematically but don't cope with the game so well because they don't read the messages carefully enough. Nicola, however, is the most interesting case. She needed considerable help in previous sessions and Norma has said she is a borderline member of the group that she is in for mathematics. I watch her playing the game and at one point she literally cannot bring herself to press the key of the computer board to bring up an answer in case it should prove to be the wrong one. Her hand is literally shaking so much that she presses the wrong key. Seeing her in this state one can only recognise it as a damning indictment of what we do to some children.
>
> (Fieldnote diary 20 May)

Both Norma and Jean, like many teachers, recognise that Nicola's behaviour is an extreme manifestation of that displayed by many children who lack confidence when asked to tackle problems. The analysis of the film episodes suggests, however, that these two teachers have each developed a different 'two-stage theory' of pedagogy about how best to increase such pupils' confidence so that they will, in time, become less dependent. The term 'two-stage theory' (Galton 1989) describes a model of teaching whereby teachers behave differently towards pupils during the initial encounters until a desired pattern has been established after which they adopt a different style. One familiar illustration of this theory concerns the advice to new teachers 'not to smile until Christmas'. When taking a new class they are urged by more experienced colleagues to be firm at first since a 'tough new teacher deserves respect' while 'a friendly new teacher is perceived as being weak'. Once the pupils have learned to respond to the teacher's authority, however, the second stage can begin during which the teacher becomes more relaxed and even shares a joke with the pupils on occasions.

Both Norma and Jean operated a two-stage theory in their efforts to maintain group activity. Norma's approach may be likened to 'guided discovery' since, at first, she worked closely with the pupils, demonstrating equipment and offering support and advice when they encountered difficulties. As will be seen, later in this section, Norma hoped that by this means pupils would develop sufficient confidence to accept more responsibility for the task as the lesson progressed. Jean, on the other hand, appeared to adopt the opposite strategy. She, appeared, quite deliberately, to withdraw her participation from the activity initially so that pupils had to rely on their peers for support. Once, however, a certain amount of collaboration had developed she became increasingly involved in the discussion by raising questions and challenging the groups conclusions.

From the analysis of the filmed episodes two further propositions emerged.

Proposition 4

The two stage approach, adopted by Norma, which seeks to guide pupils initially, leaving them to take more responsibility at a later stage, fosters a pupil's individual identity within the group at the expense of social identity. Such an approach tends, therefore, to result in *co-operative activity* whereby each pupil in the group assumes personal responsibility for a particular part of the joint task.

Proposition 5

An approach, such as that used by Jean, which initially stresses the autonomy of the group tends to foster pupil's social identity at the expense of their individual identities.

Such groups tend to engage in *collaborative activity* where individual pupils make a contribution to a single outcome as part of a joint task.

In Norma's case, during the introduction to the lesson on making a timer (p. 96) it may be remembered that pupils were told not to 'dive in and get cracking straight away'. Later they were told also to have a good careful look and 'see what you have got in your tray and then start to apply the task'.

Norma then invites questions to clarify that the children have understood the task.

Pupil   Can you make any sort of timer?

Norma   It's completely up to you, Michael, because as I always say you have much better ideas than I have. Sometimes you surprise me with some of the things that you can suggest.

Pupil   Can you use as much of anything as you want?

Norma   Completely. You have got the whole range. There is paper, the whole lot, everything is there. If you need anything else, say from your cookery area, just go down there and collect it.

Norma then sets about directing the pupils to specific places so that the groups move off the carpeted area one at a time. There is much chatter as the pupils begin to get out and inspect the materials but Norma calls for attention and then says,

Norma   Right, listen, stop a minute. Before you start I am not going to come round for the first couple of minutes. I'll let you get talking to each other. I don't want to interfere so what I want you to do is to talk. Don't come to me. I'll just stand and watch and then come to you later as you have got into it.

In spite of these instructions, that the pupils are to spend time discussing the task with each other, the digital clock on the film shows that only thirty seconds have elapsed before the following dialogue occurs. Norma has been standing next to one of the tables and becomes concerned at the way some of the pupils seem to be going to use their candle.

Norma   Right. Stop. Just one thing. When you are actually using a candle make sure you are safe with it. For goodness

100

Pupil   sake I don't want a fire on my hands that I have to put out. I'll light it. Be sensible about what you place your candle in.

Pupil   Is that OK?

Norma   Lovely. That's the idea Mike. Right.

Pupil   Can you make holes in this (pointing to a rubber cork)?

Norma   Don't you know how to do that? There is a pair of scissors. There you are (finding them in the tray). Never be beaten.

Norma   (Standing next to another group) Am I putting you off?

Pupil   You said you could use wire for this (pointing to the candle).

Norma   Yes, that is very sensible. Tell me about your ideas then.

Pupil   One idea is to see how long it takes to boil a bowl of water and then we will find out how much for two minutes.

Later in the lesson a group of pupils try to make a device like an egg timer. The idea is to take two yoghurt pots and to make a hole in each bottom. The two yoghurt pots are then joined so that the sand can pass between the first and the second. Norma arrives at the group's table and the following extended dialogue occurs.

Norma   Right. What is it you're after Jason? (Jason has brought a yoghurt pot and is showing Norma that he wants to find some way of making a better hole in the bottom.) Shall I show you how to do it? I'll want a hammer and a nail. I can do that thing but go and get me the matches then. Oh, they are just there behind Bobby.

Pupil   (on the same table) Can I start to stick this on further? The plasticine.

Norma   Yes. Plasticine. (And then, turning to Jason.) Is that the size of hole you want then?

Jason   Yes.

Norma   Do you want the same here (pointing to the second yoghurt pot)?

Jason   Yes, please.

Norma   Do you want this taking out? Shall I just start you off?

Jason   We are going to put that on top of the other.

Norma   If I hit my finger your life won't be worth living.

Jason   And that one on the top towards the inside.

Norma   Yes, Yes. What then are you going to use?

Jason	And that one, we want to hold it up and start it spinning round and round for two minutes.
Norma	So you are going to spin that one. So you are going to need some kind of harness out of this string and hold it up. Ah! (Jason shows her the harness that another boy has made.) You beat me to it. It's lovely.
Jason	And on the bottom we have sellotaped it because it was leaking.
Norma	Oh, I see. Out of the edges of the cap.
Jason	Yeah, and it will start to make a pattern and see how long it will do it for.
Norma	Yes. I am not sure how it will actually time two minutes but I like your idea.
Jason	On this one we're going to put some water on the top and watch it run in.
Norma	I see. This is a different timer.
Jason	We have not tried it yet.
	(There are sounds of hammering as Norma continues to make the hole in the yoghurt pot throughout this conversation.)
Norma	It's you lot who have done CDT [Craft Design and Technology] not me.
Pupil	We are thinking of doing something with a spring but we can't think of anything. Have we got a meccano set?
Norma	Meccano? We have got metal pans. Help yourself in the cookery area. (Continuous hammering sound.) I see what you mean. (To Jason – a reference to the difficulty of making the hole.) Clever clogs here, I can't do it. I have made a little hole. I've started you off.
Jason	That one (pointing to another carton) has got a split in it. I was thinking of sellotaping it back up.
Norma	No. I think you're better off (looking at the one that Jason has done). You're better than me. I don't know what I am flapping about. I give up. (Then to another pupil who has joined the group.) Yes . . . ah! There you are. I'm just coming Theresa.

In this long exchange with Jason's group we can examine several attributes of Norma's style. Each person in Jason's group has take on responsibility for building a different timing device. There is the yoghurt pot egg timer, the device which will spin round, there is the water device and finally the proposal to use a meccano set and a spring. Jason is the leader. Norma at this stage gives much evaluative feedback. She not only offers advice on procedures such as how to light and mount the candle but also demonstrates how to make the hole in the yoghurt pot and gives opinions about some of the pupil's ideas suggesting, for example, they will need a harness to suspend the rotating device and then appearing surprised by the fact that they have already thought of it themselves. Her manner is very jokey with the children, as, for example, when she tells them that their life will not be worth living if she hits her finger with the hammer. Towards the end of the sequence other children are forming a queue around the table and before leaving to help Theresa she offers encouragement to Jason by telling him that he has done a better job with the hammer and nail than she has. His yoghurt pot, rather than the one prepared by Norma, should therefore be used to make the egg timer.

In the post-lesson interview the pressure which this style of teaching creates is discussed.

Me   Towards the end of the lesson you were under quite a lot of pressure, weren't you, with children wanting you? As they develop the work they got so many ideas going that they seemed to want you a lot and there was a problem of how to cope with these demands.

Norma   I don't think I actually solved it because there were one or two tables that I was very conscious of not having had any dealings with. I couldn't get round to them and the groups that took my time, the ones that had lots of ideas going and wanted to try them all at once, they demanded my attention and it was very difficult.

Me   Throughout you seemed very concerned to reassure the children that you liked their ideas, giving them plenty of encouragement. Was that a deliberate strategy?

Norma   Yes. I wanted to make them feel that it didn't matter that whatever they devised, even if it didn't work, it was all part of the process. I think that is very important. It is very difficult to get them out of the way of believing that there is always a right answer and a wrong answer, to get them away from that idea that there may be two right answers to encourage that kind of thinking.

Me   Do you have any strategy for doing that?

Norma   Just praise and encouragement and giving them help
        initially in situations like problem solving activities
        where they can experience that there may be two right
        answers.

Me   Like banging nails in and so on.

Norma   (laughing) Yes, which I didn't do very successfully.

Me   Is there a way of trying to reduce this pressure?

Norma   I am not sure. I think again it is part of a development.
        Eventually they will become more skilled and they will
        not require me for things like that. It is all part of this
        growing independence that we are trying to achieve.

In Jean's lessons, however, the approach was very different. We
have seen that in her introduction to making the timing device
she places less emphasis on the construction and more on the
processes of working together (p. 95). In the other lesson where
the children engage in the use of different artistic mediums to
illustrate movement she tells the pupils at the start of the lesson
that she has issued them with biros and not pencils for making
the initial sketches,

> Because I don't want you to be frightened and think 'Oh,
> I'm going to make a mistake. I must rub it out.' Because you
> are not on about that. It doesn't matter. Trying to
> understand the shape that the models have made with their
> bodies is the more important thing.'

And later, in this introduction she continues,

> You can go off the end of the paper. So don't be frightened
> to make a big frame round it. You can go right off the edge
> and you can either concentrate on a single body part, legs,
> the arm, or the whole thing and you can ask the models to
> move for you and hold certain positions. If the paper is too
> big for you think. 'Ah! You are scared of using that. Put the
> trimmer on the side there and start.'

And in the subsequent interview Jean explains what lay behind
these instructions.

Me   One thing that was quite interesting and that perhaps you
        would like to talk about is the amount of time you spent
        reassuring and encouraging the children at the beginning.

You continually use phases like, 'Don't be frightened of this
and don't worry if it doesn't work.' Was that important?

Jean Very important.

Me Why?

Jean Because they need to get away from this sort of rut – that
right answers of things being right is important or that they
are scared of telling their idea. They need to know that they
can prove their skill by just trying something so that they
can get away from the fear that children have. Kids have
different levels and they need not always compare themselves with other children or compete with each other.
What I thought was nice in the groups was one boy who
was quite emotionally disturbed, who really couldn't
handle this sort of theme and who is actually being
encouraged by another kid, you know, to get the board a bit
closer, 'Try this, push it a certain way'. And the nice thing
was that he actually was proud although what he had
made didn't resemble any of the other things that the other
children had been doing or link in with the theme but he
wanted to say that piece of clay was his and it was important to him. I think this idea of nurturing that kind of value
in what you do is very important so I have tried to foster it
all the time. That's part and parcel of how I want things.

Me So that was a very explicit thing that you were doing. You
were saying to the pupils, 'Have a go. Don't worry if things
go wrong.' Are there other ways in your work that you try
to encourage them to do these kinds of things on their own?

Jean Perhaps it didn't come out in the film so much but in
everyday teaching I put myself at risk more often. I would
try to show myself failing at times or struggling with things
and then I would try to tell them how I feel.

Like Norma, Jean is also conscious that the pupils do not like
risking failure. However, her strategy is not to show them what
to do but to allow the pupils to see her taking similar risks and to
explain to them how she feels about the experience. When
working in this way there is increased likelihood of interactions
involving 'critical feedback' where children and teachers exchange ideas. This cannot happen initially until children have
gained sufficient confidence otherwise they will perceive the
teacher's ideas as 'a model' to be copied. The lesson in which the

children make drawings of still life models is revealing because in the subsequent interview Jean explains an important element in her strategy for building this confidence. Recognising that there is a risk when the pupils work without her support she attempts to reduce this risk by setting limits to the task. Thus, if they are anxious about making a big sketch on the paper with their biros they can either draw a large border to reduce the size or else they can cut a section off with the trimmer and can attempt first a small part of the body such as an arm or a leg.

NON-VERBAL BEHAVIOUR WITH GROUPS

Another important difference is reflected in the way that both teachers physically interact with the groups. Whereas we have described Norma as staying close to the group to encourage and, on occasions, to assist with the work, Jean holds back from such contact, particularly at the beginning of the lesson. In the lesson in which the pupils made a timing device, for example, Jean's behaviour differed from that of Norma in two particular ways. Whereas, within the first half minute Norma had begun to interact with a group, during the first three minutes of Jean's lesson no contact was made.

Subsequently, when joining the group for the next ten minutes only low levels of verbal interaction were observed. In the original ORACLE Pupil Record, the category *Teacher Present* was coded when the teacher was physically able to touch a child sitting at a table. If the teacher was present and interacting non-verbally with the child then there were several categories including *watching, listening* and *demonstrating*. Comparing the first five minutes of Norma's and Jean's lessons on making a timing device, using a five second time interval, the *teacher present* ratio between Norma and Jean was 32:10 so that Jean's contact with pupils was approximately two-thirds less. In terms of teacher–pupil interaction the ratio was 34:4 so that conversations between Jean and the groups of pupils were nearly nine times less frequent over the first five minutes following the initial intro-duction, when the pupils commenced the activity in their groups.

This difference was subsequently discussed with Jean.

Me   One of the things I noticed and wondered about was that you spent quite a lot of time, particularly at the beginning of the lesson, in what I might call, 'neutral space'. It appeared as if you did not wish to invade the children's privacy, their area around the tables, but when talking to them you did so from positions where the conversation was directed at everyone and not just at one group. Was this something that you were conscious of?

Jean   Yes. I am particularly conscious of that just now because I have spent quite a lot of time trying to stand back, watching and trying not to say trivial things like, 'That's nice' or 'That's good'.

Me   I also thought that it was interesting that when you eventually did join the group you didn't talk with them. You seem to emphasise this by the way you sat with your back half turned away from them as if you were partly with them and partly not with them. At one point on the film you actually put your hand across your mouth and watching you on the monitor you seemed to be sending the message, 'I'm not talking, I'm just watching'. Was that also deliberate or was it something that just happened?

Jean   Well, I don't know. I think it was deliberate thinking about it now. I mean, it is hard to say but I think it was. I would be inclined to behave like that naturally.

Me   Well, it certainly seemed to work because they went on and on discussing and you were just there listening to them.

Jean   Yes, just watching an activity like that you can make so many assumptions about how they are coping with things. They told me so much about their real development. How much they really knew about their ideas. At some points I was desperately wanting to encourage them by suggesting they could do it a lot easier. That way I could have ended the lesson in five minutes. If I had told them. But what is interesting for me was to realise at which stage they were actually at when it came down to them making their own decision. For me, it is so important to hear what they are saying and to listen and watch how they are coping. I can get a much clearer idea of what they are doing by the words they use, the actions they use. I feel it is important that is not just the sort of task or the end product that I judge their work by. If I can actually listen to what they have said but I must admit that it is very important to me rather than kind of keeping in dipping in all over the place and taking over.

Me   Another thing I noticed, whether it was a conscious thing or not is that when you were talking to them you got down to their level. I mean physically. You get down to their level at the table. Is this again something you think is important? Or that you do consciously?

Jean   Yes. I try to sit there in the middle for as long as possible and I sit quietly and allow them naturally to talk to each other around me until they happen to notice me and then they can decide if there is something they want from me.

Me   But you did restrict their freedom. For example, the biros. You told them they had to use biros and black paper. How do you decide when you will choose and when the children are going to be allowed to decide?

Jean   I think there ought to be times for big choices for pupils to make but there are also occasions when I narrow it down. I thought it would be a good way of getting through to the children about what was required so they could focus their attention and not become worried about having to do such a large task. It's a strategy I adopt quite often deliberately. Limiting their resources, for example, but making them understand that it is up to them how they actually interpret what they are seeing which I think is the important thing. That they should have the freedom in that aspect of it.

Me   That's quite interesting because a lot of teachers would see giving pupils initial choices as being the important things and you're saying, I don't want to put words into your mouth, but the way they actually go about the task is more important than choosing what task to do.

Jean   Yes, that's it exactly. I really do often limit children to a colour or a size at times but if they are desperate, if they reject it, then OK. I quite often do it so that they can explore as much as they can within these constraints.

Thus, in different ways, both teachers seek to increase the confidence of their pupils so that they are prepared to take risks. However, in Jean's case there is more evidence that they are also prepared to exchange their ideas with each other and to subject them to critical scrutiny. Norma hopes to increase the pupils' confidence by letting them see that they can do tasks as well as her. Jean, on the other hand, refuses help at first but deliberately limits the complexity of the task so that pupils can achieve some success by themselves in small steps.

The difference in approaches can be observed during the film by the different body language which both teachers use. Thus Norma maintains a close presence with most of the groups, there is much touching of the pupils and also examination of their work which is often praised. Jean, on the other hand, initially stands aloof from the pupils. She does not directly address them, even when she sees things which are going wrong. In a similar situation when Norma saw that there was a problem in mounting a candle she immediately joined the group and used their difficulties as an example to the rest of the class about being careful with matches. In a similar situation, Jean does not directly address the pupils but stands somewhere in the middle of the room (what I termed in the interview 'neutral space') and having observed some pupils attempting to make a timing device by burning a piece of string she calls for attention and then says,

> I have been coming around watching and looking at your ideas and I see there is a number of problems concerning the string as a way of timing two minutes. In a minute I would like to get your different ideas but I have got some of my own which you may like to think about too.

Thus, rather than directing attention to the problems of a particular group she implies that the problem is one affecting a number of different pupils. When eventually joining a group she appears, probably unconsciously, to send signals that she is there to listen rather than talk by the way she sits and also, quite dramatically at times, by placing the hand over her mouth, thus signalling her intention to remain silent.

Both methods achieve success in different ways. In Norma's class however the tendency is for each pupil within the group to make their own timing device only calling upon the aid of other pupils to help with practical tasks such as holding the plastic lemonade bottle while water is poured into it. As a result, Norma finds herself having to deal with six or seven groups tackling the same topic in thirty individual ways. As she remarks at the end of the interview she was unable to get around to all the pupils during the time available. Nevertheless, the children do gradually become less dependent over a period of time greater than that allowed for in the film episode. In the earlier example, taken from the diary, where children were engaged in experiments with soil samples, the fieldnotes chart this progress over time. One week into the project, for example, I report that,

> The afternoon passes very quickly with the children working hard. The soil groups begin to show results. We plot bar charts of the weight of soil which passes through the sieve in different samples. Some of the children sort the leaves, make diagrams and are attempting to draw up a classification. But I often have to suggest that they should try to work more together and not try to cover every leaf themselves. Even when they decide to distribute the tasks around the group the conversation tends to be of the kind expressed by Leigh, 'Well, I'm doing the Sycamore'. The same is true of the group of boys who are making models of various mini-beasts that they have discovered. Because each is working on their own the final display will not look very effective because they have used different proportions.
>
> (Fieldnote diary 8 May)

By the beginning of the fourth week, however, the responses of the children are becoming less dependent. At one point, because I have to go back to the University for a day, I show one of the children how to do some calculations on the soil samples, leaving her to instruct the others. On my return the fieldnote reports that,

> Norma is very pleased because what looked terrible in the beginning is now turning out quite well as the children start to display their own work. I know that initially she was feeling insecure because the display in Jean's class, master-minded by a student teacher, was much more creative. Along one wall this student had put a large strip of green paper to depict the river and had designed water lilies to grow out of the top. The children had cut shapes out of the green paper and stuck their creatures into the vacant space so that it looked as if their creatures were swimming in the water. In contrast, Norma's class display is not so dramatic. However, the idea for the river has come from the student teacher's files which have been supplied by the Polytechnic. It's all very pretty and there is a lot of the children's own work in it but you find a heavy sense of direction which is

not present in the display masterminded by Norma's children. I am amazed by the presentation and discussion which I am able to sit in with just before lunch. The children, initially, are clearly very worried about making what they call a 'speech' to the rest of the class and they generally prefer to read out something that they have written but the discussion that follows is quite spontaneous and they raise issues such as whether worms have eyes, where the soil goes when they push it out of the way, what beetles eat and the soil group describe, very vividly, their discovery that most of the moisture is found in the twigs and leaves in the top soil and that differences disappear when this debris had been sieved out.

The children listen to each other attentively and ask each other interesting questions. The atmosphere is relaxed and easy with only one or two pushes and nudges from Bret and Richard.

(Fieldnote diary 22 May)

There do, however, appear to be important differences between Norma's and Jean's approaches. In Norma's case, although the children do move, eventually, to take greater control of the learning, it is noticeable that during their planning of group work, in almost every case, they work co-operatively rather than collaboratively. Thus in both the timer experiment and in the art lesson the children tended to produce individual products and to combine these into a group display as illustrated by my diary comment (p. 110) where the children made their creatures to a different scale and where I continually record my frustration at the children's reluctance to reflect more carefully on what were are doing.

Jean's approach might be described as providing *freedom within a framework*. She makes it clear that she expects the children to discuss and work collaboratively together but, recognising the risks involved, limits the range of issues or activities with which they are confronted. She argues that this makes them more confident and, as a result, they tend to engage in more collaborative activity where they share abstract ideas and where they work together towards one joint outcome.

RELATIONSHIPS

The cartoon pictures were dominated by the comments from teachers on aspects of pupils' behaviour. Most of these teachers' comments were perceived to be negative in tone and were often linked to situations where pupils had either produced incorrect answers or failed to finish work. In the subsequent interview with pupils at Burwood this issue produced the strongest reaction so that at one point the tape had to be turned off because otherwise it would not have been possible to have played it back to the staff. Pupils claimed that they never knew where they were with teachers, that one minute everything was allright and the next 'they were shouting at you'. This created a situation where it was better not to take risks by volunteering answers to a teacher's questions unless absolutely necessary. One favoured pupil strategy was to draw the teacher into discussion until she made clear what was required. Implementing this strategy would be difficult in Jean's class since she deliberately chose, at the beginning of a new activity, where there was greatest uncertainty, not to offer children clues of this kind. It was, therefore, significant that in the interview Mrs Wright was singled out as an exception to the children's general complaint about the behaviour of teachers. It would seem that to develop the style of work which Jean achieved in her classroom it was also necessary for her to create a relationship which allowed children to feel safe when they were engaged in risk taking activities, such as problem solving and abstract discussion.

This view is supported by other teachers. In Jennifer Nias's (1989) study of teachers at work, those interviewed claimed that informal learning came about only when they ceased to be 'the teacher, the boss figure, the policeman' and become 'relaxed and not frightened any more'. These teachers also talked about 'feeling cared for' by the pupils in the same way that the pupils in the interview felt that Jean Wright 'cared for them'. This notion of mutual caring and concern leads to the final proposition.

Proposition 6

Collaborative group work, requires a 'relaxed' classroom ethos where both teachers and pupils feel that their needs are recognised and cared for. For this ethos to develop teachers and pupils need, on occasions, to consider more than the 'surface' behaviour (e.g. noisy class, pupil not paying attention, etc.) and explore the reasons for such behaviour together with the feelings which may have prompted it.

Dealing with pupil behaviour at a 'surface' level only tends to force teachers into being the 'boss figure' and it seems that pupils find it very difficult to judge the moment when teachers decide to abandon this role, as the following extract from the interview with pupils at Burwood illustrates.

First boy	If you are in a group and you are all writing out different things for about half an hour she comes up and says, 'How much have you done?' and you say, 'Nothing' and you get done and we are discussing really.
First girl	You don't always get done for a single word you say.
Second girl	A lot of things like you'll not get done for like you would sometimes argue with the teacher about what you were doing and she won't tell you off because you are arguing a point of view and you want to tell it to her.
Third girl	But when we were playing with Miss Stone she told us to prove it and she told this girl to tell her teacher and when she did tell the teacher she got told off for it.
First boy	Like we have to go to give evidence.

Here we see a common dilemma for pupils particularly in group discussion where they are expected to argue for their point of view but from the way they argue earn a rebuke from the teacher on the grounds that they are 'answering back'. Jean, however, seems to have found a way out of this dilemma although she admits it is a risk.

Perhaps it didn't come out in the film so much but in every day teaching I would perhaps put myself at risk more than I did. Show myself failing at times or struggling at things and tell the children *how I feel about it*. Lead by example, myself really.

There is strong evidence from both the diary and from the film that Jean consistently adopted this strategy. In her introduction to the lesson on making a timing device she tells the children.

Don't just do things and then ignore others – I hate that when I am working in a group with someone. I am stood there like a kind of lemon and I have not got a clue what they are doing because they have not explained it to me. So if you have got an idea, explain it to your group. Try things out together. If things go wrong you will all learn by your mistakes. Allright? That's very important.

Elsewhere when Jean deals with an incident in the diary field-notes a similar approach is described.

This morning in Jean's class there was a fight between a boy and a girl whose names I didn't know because I haven't had much contact with them. I was passing by at the time and heard the children complaining that Bret had hit Lisa and that Lisa was crying. . . . Jean just brought the children together and asked what it was about. It emerged that Bret had been teasing Lisa about another boy. She had lashed out and he had hit her much harder in response. Although Jean made clear her disapproval of the behaviour she immediately moved from dealing with the two pupils and opened a discussion with the others by saying how difficult it was at this age to cope with one's feelings about the opposite sex. She then told them about an incident in her own life when she was 11 and how she felt embarrassed and felt her face going red when her mother had made remarks about a boy cousin in front of other adults.

(Fieldnote diary 20 May)

In these ways the children come to accept that in their dealings with her she will be fair because they also feel that she understands what motivates them to act in the way that they do. Because of this they are also prepared to respect Jean's feelings particularly her strong stance on race. During the interview, for example, it was said,

Boy Pupil   The teachers ask you if you want to work on race and about coloureds and sometimes we are scared to say something like when people keep calling them names and that but Mrs Wright is against that sort of stuff because she wouldn't like someone to call her a name like that. So we don't do it.

114

Clearly, all teachers try to work towards establishing the kinds of relationships where they are relaxed and the children feel secure. One of the main ways in which this mutual trust develops is through the sharing of information about each other. Thus Norma, in her introduction to the lesson on making a timing device, tells a story of her own young daughter who is becoming increasingly aware of time because she wishes to know when her favourite TV programmes will be on. She then goes on to tell another story about an American lady who telephoned her at one o'clock in the morning because she couldn't work out the difference in the time-zones between the United States and Britain. Although the actual story is somewhat confusing, in that making a two-minute timer has little to do with working out the differences in time-zones, it is introduced, presumably, as a way of making everyone feel more relaxed about the task which the pupils have to undertake. It is Norma's way of getting the children to stop seeing her as, what Nias's (1989) teachers argue they don't want to be, 'the teacher, the boss figure'.

In return the pupils respond, sharing their secrets with the teacher which in turn helps the teacher to understand the children better. The following fieldnote, taken from the diary, conveys something of my own developing relationship with Norma's class.

The last part of the afternoon tells you something of the rewards of teaching. The children are continuing with the design of various leaves, animals and roots which they have collected in the wood and are now sewing on the hessian backing. I get the worm I am sewing and am invited by Leigh and Rachael to sit with them. However, remembering how nice and attractive it is to feel wanted, I make a point of getting up from time to time in order to join other groups. Leigh has drawn a beetle but doesn't like it so she makes the decision to get rid of the first drawing and do it again. I applaud her for this and tell her about Indian artists who sometimes draw the same Buddha over and over. This gets us into the subject of reincarnation and we speculate as to whether her beetle was one of her ancestors.

We are now joined by two others, Debbie and Clare, and as we work on our sewing we chat together. We ask each other about textures and colours and Leigh has the ability to do very compact stitching so she takes over my worm and helps with my rather amateurish effort. They tell me about Michelle who is going out with Bevan (a handsome boy). I ask what going out means and they laugh and say 'going to discos together and things'. There is silence while we work and then Debbie volunteers the information that he really fancied her but she doesn't like him. 'We had to send him a note telling him that Michelle fancied him.' Then Leigh says rather scornfully, 'They do kissing and things'. I tell them that this is all a surprise to me since I didn't have a girlfriend until I left school. They clearly doubt this.

(Fieldnote diary 8 May)

There is, however, a difference between what takes place in the above exchange and those described earlier involving Jean Wright. I tell the children about myself without disclosing in any way how I felt about not having a girlfriend, unlike Jean, who in a similar exchange, tells the pupils of her embarrassment when her mother referred to the idea of her cousin and herself 'carrying on'.

Most teachers, perhaps because they have been told during training that 'a friendly new teacher will be perceived by pupils as weak' tend to fight shy of the kind of openness displayed by Jean, although they are prepared to let children have a glimpse of other aspects of their lives outside the classroom, particularly when this involves their own children or their own childhood. But the principles advanced during their training, that 'pupils need strict limits on their freedom' and that children wish teachers to be 'firm but fair', often create situations where teachers oscillate between being the 'boss figure' and being 'relaxed' in these ways. This was the case with some teachers at Burwood, as illustrated by the following incident in the first year base area.

I am interested in the approach that Pat and Mary have. Both are very kind but partly because it is coming near to half term and the children seem restive they are much sharper than either Norma or Jean in terms of discipline. Before we go out to do our sketching, there are constant reminders about behaving well when we are outside school in order to keep up its good name. Some children are told off because they have turned their backs or are not listening. It's all done kindly but there is no reasoning with the

116

children, as with Jean, and by the time that all the instructions have been given and have been interrupted by various reprimands half an hour of the afternoon has gone and it has started raining. In two minutes it is raining so hard we have to take off our anoraks and decide to go out to do our sketching on another day.

We prepare the base area for sketching and the teachers spend a lot of time sorting children into groups so we lose nearly another quarter of an hour of the session. Although the children appear to listen attentively to the instructions, as soon as we start the same thing happens as with Norma's class in the wood episode. Once they are sat down at tables their enthusiasm gets the better of them and they begin to cover the paper with badly proportioned drawings without even looking at their rough sketches. Some children have not even bothered to do a rough sketch and, instead, rush at the task in order to finish it with the result that the houses have squat, narrow, ill-proportioned shapes and crooked windows and vast doors which are nearly half the size of the building. It takes the best part of the lesson to get round and see that everyone is settled.

(Fieldnote diary 6 May)

Here the fieldnote is written from the point of view of a detached observer. The emphasis rapidly switches, however, when this observer becomes a central participant.

Now I begin to have a really hateful afternoon. It starts badly in that I mistake the instructions which Mary gives me when she says, 'They are all yours'. I tell the children to turn towards me and at the same time Pat is telling them to split into three groups because there is a remedial maths group which will go off. The children begin to laugh and I think it is because I have given them one instruction and Pat has given them another. Only afterwards does a pupil come up and tell me that they were laughing because Matthew had 'trumped'. However, the damage is done because for the rest of the afternoon several of the other children see if they can also 'trump' so that they can produce another hiatus.

For the reading period they divide into smaller groups. Unfortunately, many of the children need new books but

Jean is in the library area with the second year group reading them a story. She says, however, that my class can change their books if they go quietly so I have to take on the role of childminder, shepherding parties of two to six to and from the gallery to change their books. I find myself now sounding exactly like Pat and Mary earlier. 'Will you listen?' I can hear my voice rising. I am now one of the team completely – a member of the club – but I have succumbed to fear. To get to the gallery I have to get the children to walk across the third year base and I want them to do it properly so that everyone will know what a good teacher I am. So I, unwittingly, take it out on the children and make them wait at the door and then make them walk towards the gallery and then wait at the door leading to the gallery until I come for them. I justify this because, like a student teacher, I argue that it is not my class and therefore I have to treat the children consistently the way Pat and Mary do.

We end the day, I suspect, on all sides feeling very smug. Me, inwardly, because I think this experience proves my point that there has to be another way of dealing with the children and no doubt both Pat and Mary because they think I now know what it is like to have to teach these kids and that maybe I'll not be so full of theory next time. Mary was working nearby when I had the children lining up to go to the library and no doubt heard my voice raise in frustration as I ask them for the umpteenth time, 'Why don't you listen?' and, indeed, asking Mark the classic question, 'What did I say a moment ago?' with him being unable to tell me.

(Fieldnote diary 22 May)

In such situations the need to be firm, particularly early on in one's relationship with children, appears paramount. But from the children's perspective, however, these boundaries cannot be so clear. The contrast between the same person sitting in the midst of children sewing and chatting about boyfriends and on another occasion telling them in a sharp voice to 'shut up and listen' requires of them that they continually test out each new situation in order to determine where they stand. With Jean's approach, the pupils do not seem to have this problem, partly because they know that she understands how they feel and will not judge their mistakes harshly. Consequently, they are prepared to engage in activities where the outcomes are unclear because they are confident that Jean will not misinterpret their faltering first efforts in negative ways.

My own attempts to develop a similar approach to that used by Jean are described more fully in Galton (1989).

Inevitably, as one shifts towards this way of working an element of uncertainty in the relationship is created and the diary records at some points the unhappiness of Norma who felt that 'my presence is loosening the control of the class' because 'you need to keep on top of some of them all the time'. But there is also evidence from the diary that, if one attempts to employ the strategies used by Jean, children with, initially, strong dependency and fear of failure begin to take risks and experiment. For example, Nicola, the girl who was too frightened to put her finger on the computer button, in case she recorded a wrong answer, was also apprehensive in the following episode.

I start with the soil people by blindfolding them and getting them to put their hands into the mixture and feel it. This produces panic amongst one or two of the girls, particularly Nicola, who says that there will be mini-beasts inside. Then comes the difficult problem of trying to reproduce these feelings into their clay models. There is plenty of frustration as the clay doesn't work but gradually we learn together how to use the material and begin to feel its plasticity. Some children opt for the tiles in which they make a collage of all the things that were found in the soil. Others construct decayed leaves. Only with Ian do I have no success. He keeps on wanting more clay and I tell him he can't have it until he has made something with what he has got. I am determined not to take over which is what he is trying to make me do. Throughout the afternoon he goes through various phases of fooling, attempting to copy the other children and finally settles on making a monkey's face which he tells me he is calling Maurice. (He has heard Norma calling my name and I suppose this is the new thing to bait me.) Just towards the end he irrationally smashes the whole thing and so ends with nothing. I think it was the other children asking him, scornfully, 'What's that, Ian?'. Oh, I forgot that in the middle of the afternoon he spent much of the time making an obscene phallic symbol but

119

fortunately his art work with clay was not yet of a sufficiently high standard to make it recognisable so it passed unnoticed with the other children.

(Fieldnote diary 14 May)

What the diary episode does not record is a conversation with Nicola about my own experience of being frightened of creatures. The incident I describe is a shocking one, namely about a small gerbil belonging to one of my children which fell from the cage and broke its back. The gerbil was making intense screeching noises and was clearly dying in considerable pain. Not being able to pick it up I took the cage outside, tipped the gerbil out and ran the car over it. With Nicola and her friends there is, at first, horror at my disclosure but we then discuss what one could do if faced with an animal in pain but not able to handle the creature. Nicola is strangely quiet but then goes away and puts her hand in the soil. Subsequently, at times when we are covering worksheets, Nicola begins to be more positive about her computation, learning to check her answers without coming out to see the teacher and beginning to experiment in her art and her writing in all sorts of exciting ways. While the same rapport was never quite attained with Ian there were moments in which greater communication between us developed, notably when I explained to him how I felt when two parents, accompanied by the deputy head, came into the classroom to find him behaving objectionably.

Not all incidents are as dramatic as those described but the need for the teacher to show pupils that he or she understands what it feels like to work in a group does seem an important element in creating a collaborative climate in the classroom.

SUMMARY OF FINDINGS

From this and the previous chapter it is possible to draw some tentative conclusions about the development of effective group work in the primary classroom.

1 The value that the teacher places on collaboration must be clearly communicated to the pupils. This is particularly important where collaborative groups are used for only a limited range of activities.
2 Children need to be taught how to collaborate by breaking

120

down activities into small-scale exercises designed to improve certain competences and skills, such as listening and handling disagreements.

3 Once these conditions have been met it also appears that it is best to begin with small practical activities where there is a specific solution to the problem rather than more open-ended problem solving. When more abstract tasks are set it would appear useful if the task can be limited so that not too many possibilities and problems need to be taken into account. Once, however, some insight has been gained into the different roles participants can play within the group and the pupils have developed a sense of group identity, then the quality and quantity of pupil–pupil interaction does not seem to depend on the nature of the class nor on the size of the group (in this study the group size ranged from two to eight but was always of mixed ability).

4 As the quantity and quality of teacher feedback given to pupils about their work increased the children worked more independently of the teacher. This feedback could be described as *critical feedback* (about the quality of the work) rather than *evaluative* feedback (which only corrected mistakes). By its nature, therefore, critical feedback tends to take place once the children have gained some confidence in their ideas so that, initially, there is a minimum of teacher–pupil interaction. Where evaluative teacher feedback is required it should be delivered to the class in general rather than to a group in particular.

5 With collaborative work of this kind (as opposed to co-operative work where children still produce individual products related to the joint outcome) the relationship with the pupils is crucial. In particular, pupils need to have confidence that the teacher understands what it feels like to work in groups so that they will not, for example, be accused of time wasting when they are, in fact, discussing.

6

GROUP WORK
From practice to theory

INTERPRETATION OF DATA

In the previous chapter a number of conclusions was drawn based upon the analysis of fieldnotes and the interactions of teachers and pupils during four video-taped lessons. In pursuing this analysis there could be, as French (1990: 42) argues, a tendency 'to ascribe more significance than is strictly speaking justified, to impute unwarranted motives and intentions to participants and then to put one's understandings forward implicitly or otherwise as the only possible way of interpreting the data'. French suggests that to avoid the danger of over-interpretation it is necessary for the researcher to produce more than one hypothesis to explain the data. She describes, as an example, some research carried out by French and French (1984) where four possible hypotheses were put forward to account for the fact that boys appeared more likely to have the rules and norms of classroom contact explained to them than girls. Teachers were asked to examine the four possible explanations and to comment on them. Drawing on this experience French (1990) argues that it may not always be possible to arrive at a definitive account which can explain such interactions although it is often likely that one of the explanations will appear more plausible to teachers than the others.

One of the problems with the approach, suggested by French, concerns the status of the explanations accepted by the participant teachers as plausible. For one thing there could be a tendency for participants, when faced with accounts of their actions, particularly in cases where such actions might be regarded as relatively unsuccessful, to attribute this behaviour to reasons which, in part absolve the participant from any responsibility. Thus in cases of disruptive behaviour by pupils, teachers may well accept poor home background as the explanation rather than the particular teaching strategy which they used to deal with the problem. Such effects of attribution theory are well documented (Weiner 1986). Thus in the incident with the first year pupils, described during the previous chapter, I attributed the failure of the lesson to the classroom ethos created by Pat and Mary rather to anything which I myself might have said or done during the exchanges with the pupils (p. 117). In such cases there are always likely to be discrepancies between the participant and observer's causal attributions. To suggest, as French does, that we should take the observer's explanation only if it accords with those of the participant teacher is to ignore the likely effects of these psychological processes.

There is, however, another approach which avoids giving too much weight to the observer's personal interpretation of the data. This alternative strategy replaces the 'within-method' triangulation procedure suggested by French (in which the accounts of participants and the observer are compared) and instead uses 'between method' triangulation (Delamont 1983) whereby two different and independent methods are compared with the observer's interpretation of the classroom data. Thus in Delamont's (1976) account of friendship patterns in a girls' direct grant school, observations made in the classroom were compared with a sociogram analysis and with the choices that pupils made when invited to meet the author in groups of three outside the school. We can modify this triangulation approach to develop the theory of teaching relating to collaborative group work, providing we can identify three different sources of data to support the hypotheses set out at the end of the previous chapter.

In his discussion of Effective Teaching in Schools Kyriacou (1986) argues that there are three fundamental ways in which we can analyse the process of teaching. The first way is what he terms a surface level of analysis. This is essentially the approach adopted by those who engage in process-product research (Gage 1985) where the behaviour of teachers and pupils in effective and ineffective classrooms are compared and significant differences identified. In the past, researchers using this approach have usually defined effectiveness solely in terms of success on standardised tests. This, however, is not a necessary limitation.

The analysis of the research results, described in Chapter 3, essentially made use of this approach. The criteria used to differentiate between ineffective and effective group work was the pupils' rankings for certain kinds of group activity. Analysis of the comments of pupils in the cartoon pictures, supported by data collected in earlier projects, based on classroom observation, was then used to draw conclusions about the kinds of interactions which distinguished effective and ineffective group work in the classroom and the positive emotional feelings which the pupils involved must develop to engage successfully in such group activity.

The second approach, suggested by Kyriacou, comes from the analysis of teachers' statements about their actions, what is often called 'craft knowledge'. It is argued that a teacher's actions are driven by certain beliefs about how learning takes place, even though some of these ideas may be difficult to articulate. Thus, in the previous chapter Jean has a problem in explaining the use she makes of body language when first joining a group although the result appears to be that the pupils did not expect her to participate in the conversation immediately she arrived to join them.

There are, however, other instances when, for example, Norma talks about 'giving them [i.e. the pupils] help initially in situations like problem solving' as 'part of a development' so that 'eventually they will become more skilled and they will not require me for things like that'. This is, in effect, a clear rationale for the use of a guided discovery approach. If the results of empirical process-product studies lead to conclusions which are in accord with the teacher's craft knowledge of teaching there are stronger grounds for feeling that the surface analysis has some degree of validity.

Kyriacou (1986), however, includes a third level of analysis which derives from attempts to identify the major psychological variables involved. Kyriacou lists a large number of psychological concepts which have been identified as underpinning aspects of effective teaching. Since the present analysis has concentrated on social rather than cognitive aspects of learning in groups the key concepts are those of pupil expectations, attitudes and self-concept. Thus, the triangulation process, recommended by Delamont (1983), can be modified by comparing the empirical data with the observer's negotiated interpretation of the explanation offered by teachers to account for their practice.

Where such interpretation is supported by the empirical data the conclusions are then checked against current psychological theory in the related area.

The purpose of the rest of this chapter is, therefore, to explore how far the analysis put forward in the previous three chapters, based largely on the empirical data or on the teachers' analysis of their own behaviour, can be reinforced by the theories which have been developed to explain what Pollard (1985) has called 'the social world of the primary classroom'. The conclusion will tend to suggest that the interpretation of these data is not idiosyncratic but can be generalised to more than the classrooms studied when establishing criteria for effective group work in the primary school.

SELF-CONCEPT AND THE PRIMARY CLASSROOM

The general impression made on a casual visit to a primary classroom is that it is a place of intense activity. In the ORACLE study (Galton *et al.* 1980) teachers were interacting with their pupils for, on average, 70 per cent of the lesson time. One group of teachers, the *infrequent changers*, raised this level of interaction to nearly 90 per cent. Thus a central feature of the typical primary classroom is the atmosphere of 'busyness' which is accentuated because the bulk of the interactions between teachers and pupils are on an individual one to one basis, and to attend to different children's needs the teacher must continually move rapidly around the classroom. If, however, our casual visitor, instead of focusing on the general atmosphere, observes particular children for periods of time a very different picture begins to emerge. There are some children who, even when left to work alone for considerable periods, maintain a high level of 'busyness'. In the ORACLE transfer study (Galton and Willcocks 1983) these pupils were named *hard grinders*. At the other extreme is a group of pupils who seem more interested in other pupils' work than in their own. They are constantly on the move and whenever they stop to see what other pupils are doing a non-task related conver- sation is likely to occur. In the ORACLE study (Galton *et al.* 1980) these pupils were called *attention seekers* since they were the focus of a considerable proportion of the teachers' individual interactions. They might have been better named *attention getters* because their behaviour often elicited a comment from the teacher, in the form

125

of either a reprimand for fooling or an exhortation to get on with their work.

More interesting was the bulk of the pupils who neither worked on their own nor engaged in the attention getting behaviour. These were the pupils who gave the appearance of working steadily but who, in reality, found ways of reducing their time on task without drawing the attention of the teacher upon themselves. One group, the *intermittent workers*, tended to work hard whenever the teacher's eyes were upon them. When the teacher was engaged elsewhere in the classroom, however, they ceased work and instead spent their time talking about other things with their fellow pupils. They would, for example, discuss the previous night's TV programmes or weekend football. Since they always appeared to be working and not talking when the teacher looked their way the latter's perception was that they were continually on task. Such pupils have been described by other researchers, for example, in Tizard *et al.*'s (1988) study where the overall level of time on task was found to be just under 49 per cent. Another group of children who engage in a different kind of task avoidance was named *easy riders* (Galton and Willcocks 1983). These pupils gave the impression of working steadily but in fact worked as slowly as possible without attracting the teacher's attention. Thus these pupils took longer than others to find the correct page in the book, longer to write their name and to draw a margin in their exercise work book. In this way they had often completed only a quarter of a page of writing when other pupils, such as the *hard grinders*, had covered one side. When this kind of behaviour was initiated at the start of a year the teacher soon came to accept that such pupils 'lacked concentration' and were therefore able to complete only a limited amount of work during any one class session. Such pupils were then often praised for their minimum efforts instead of being encouraged to extend their ideas further. Over time, therefore, teachers tended to set them less demanding tasks in the belief that these pupils were 'slow' learners.

Such behaviours are part of what has been termed 'exchange bargains' by the American sociologist, Howard Becker, who studied the working of the American College system. He found that freshmen allowed their instructors to perform effectively, thus giving the appearance of being in control, but at the cost of only setting work from which all the students could achieve satisfactory grades (Becker *et al.* 1968). According to Pollard (1985; 1987) primary classrooms in Britain exhibit similar features. Pollard argues that there exists in the primary classroom a 'working consensus' consisting of 'shared social understandings between the teacher and the pupils which structure and frame the classroom climate in terms of routines, conventions and expectations' (Pollard 1987: 177). For Pollard this working consensus is achieved by a series of negotiations, mostly covert, by which the various participants attempt to achieve their 'interests at hand'.

In Becker's study the freshmen's 'interests at hand' were largely determined by the need to achieve satisfactory grades so that they could remain in college. In the primary classroom, however, until the advent of the National Curriculum and standard assessment tasks, there has been little emphasis on formal grading and the perceived distinctions in the level of performance between one pupil and another are far more subtle. According to Pollard (1987) the pupils' 'interests at hand' represent the 'various facets of self which are juggled in the ebb and flow of classroom processes to produce an overall level of satisfaction' (Pollard 1987: 179). Interests at hand, therefore, are primarily concerned with the maintenance of self-image and the retention of personal dignity which is closely linked to the way in which pupils are viewed by both their teachers and their peers.

Pollard (1985) has also classified pupils into various groupings. Pollard's pupils belong to either the goodies, the jokers or the gang. Goodies placed much importance on the way they were perceived by their teachers and therefore conform totally to the working consensus. They might be likened to the *hard grinders* in the ORACLE study. Gangs, on the other hand, often because they had learning difficulties, tended to stress the importance of peer group membership and were often prepared to reject the working consensus for the sake of group popularity. There were, therefore, some similarities between these pupils and the ORACLE *attention getters*. Jokers, on the other hand, tried to get the best of both worlds being prepared sometimes to have a laugh during lessons at the teacher's expense although never to such an extent that it earned the teacher's disapproval. They fit into the pattern of the *intermittent workers* and *easy riders*, the bulk of the pupils in the ORACLE study. Other researchers have also identified groups of children who have similar characteristics. Bennett (1976), for example, classifies pupils as saints and

127

sinners. These pupils would be similar to Pollard's goodies and gangs. Measer and Woods (1984) identified pupils as knife edgers while Holt (1984: 91) has described pupils as fence straddlers. This latter group was very similar to Pollard's jokers whose success lay in their skill and flexibility when attempting to bridge both types of social system so that they were able 'to square their reference groups in both systems in ways which goodies do not attempt and which gangs would not attempt' (Pollard 1987: 179).

There is, therefore, ample evidence to sustain the existence of different types of pupil behaviour within the primary classroom. In Pollard's views these behaviours are a manifestation of the pupils' attempt to maintain their self-esteem thereby enhancing their self-concept. Such terms are often used interchangeably by many writers but Burns (1982) defines the self-concept as composed of 'all the beliefs and evaluations an individual has about him/herself'. In each important aspect of people's lives individuals will have a belief about themselves (the self-image) and an evaluation of this belief (their self-esteem). The self-concept is, therefore, a global judgement based upon these individual self-images and self-esteem. I might believe that I am doing badly on a worksheet because the pupil next to me has done ten questions and I have done only five (self-image). As a result I may come to a decision that I am no good at mathematics (self-esteem). This then extends to other areas of the curriculum. I may then regard myself, generally, as a poor student (self-concept). As a result I indulge in certain types of behaviour that avoid having to demonstrate to the teacher whether I can finish my work satisfactorily.

There is very little disagreement that one of the major ingredients of pupils' self-concept is their academic self-image. However, there is considerable debate about whether academic achievement is the cause or the effect of a person's self-concept. At one extreme the argument runs that pupils' self-confidence and their self-esteem are enhanced by success, while others argue that by interaction with the teacher pupils' self-confidence and hence their self-worth can be built up to a point where they want to perform in ways which match their teacher's expectations of them.

In the previous chapter we saw that Norma and Jean tended, in their approach to group work, to represent these two extreme positions. Norma was inclined to the view that achievement

128

improved self-confidence and hence ultimately the pupil's self-concept. She, therefore, concentrated on giving them as much help as needed in the early part of the lesson in the belief that once pupils had achieved something of value they would improve their self-esteem and develop the confidence to work independently of her. Jean, on the other hand, devoted her initial efforts to building up the pupils' self-confidence in their own worth. By deliberately minimising the value which she placed upon success, by arguing that it was trying out ideas rather than completing the task which was important, she encouraged the children to take risks in their learning. In contrast to Norma she kept her interactions to a minimum allowing pupils to develop a sense of ownership in their activities in the hope that, as their belief in themselves developed, their self-esteem would prove strong enough to withstand her constructive criticisms of their achievements.

Researchers such as Kutnick (1988), however, argue that the building up of a pupil's academic self-concept is a more complex process than suggested by either view. For most children it is a combination derived from the teacher's interventions and the pupils' performance, particularly in high-status subject areas such as English and mathematics. In particular, specific self-concepts, relating to the main subject areas of the curriculum are, according to Schunk (1990), far less crystallised than general academic self-concept. Bandura (1982), for example, argues that a person's belief about their capabilities to engage in activities necessary to attain designated performance levels, a pupil's self-efficacy (closely linked to self-esteem) is highly likely to influence choice of activities. Thus, in the opening paragraphs of the first chapter the pupil who avoided participating in any group work by opting to take the part of the dead pilot would likely hold a low sense of self-efficacy as a member of the group, whereas the other pupils clearly believed that they were capable of participating in a useful manner. Self-efficacy also affects motivation so that, when they encounter difficulties, pupils who believe that they are capable of working in a group will persist longer and develop better skills than those who doubt their ability to collaborate. Schunk (1990) also argues that when dealing with domain specific self-concepts then training programmes that include not only instruction but also opportunities to practise particular skills tend to increase the pupils' self-confidence. In particular, positive feedback enhances these feelings of self-efficacy but this increase will be short-lived if pupils' subsequent efforts turn out poorly. Hence the need, initially, to reduce the complexity of the task, as Jean Wright did, in order to ensure that pupils can achieve partial success.

In summary, therefore, this evidence suggests that the guided discovery approach, adopted by Norma, can be of value in developing pupils' general academic self-concept. However, for more specific achievements as, for example, learning to work effectively within a group, the research evidence suggests that Jean's approach, of first providing training opportunities to develop the necessary skills and then restricting conditions so they are likely to ensure success for the maximum number of pupils, is the more effective strategy. At the same time, it is necessary for teachers to make clear to pupils that they place great value on the performance of these skills, otherwise, although students may judge themselves competent they will derive no pride in their achievements which will then have a resulting negligible effect on their self-esteem. Again, therefore, the positive effects of Jean's emphasis on the importance and the value that she placed upon collaboration appears to be supported by the research literature.

TASK DEMANDS IN THE COLLABORATIVE CLASSROOM

In the previous section we examined the problems faced by pupils when asked to participate in groups. For some children such activities can seem threatening as pupils lack confidence in their ability to exercise the skills required and because the goals of such collaboration are unclear. Such pupils with little self-confidence regularly seek to avoid placing themselves in a position where they have to demonstrate their capability (or lack of it). For the teacher, however, self-esteem is closely bound up with the ability to motivate a class of pupils to perform the set task adequately. To be able to demonstrate this ability in ways which are recognised by colleagues is important and, since the other teachers are usually not present when the task is taking place, it is the outcome of that task which must provide tangible evidence of a teacher's success. For this reason researchers, such as Anderson and Burns (1990), have argued that the central concept in the study of teaching should be the instructional task. In their view it is the task rather than a teacher's personal beliefs about the teaching methods which determines the content of the lesson and how it is taught in that classroom. They cite, as evidence in support of their view, observational studies which show that the strategies used to teach mathematical computation are very similar regardless of the fact that the teacher tends to adopt a traditional class approach or favours an approach based upon individualised learning.

In much of the literature, however, tasks have generally been characterised solely in terms of the intellectual demands which they make upon pupils. Following the development of Bloom *et al.*'s (1956) *Taxonomy of Educational Objectives*, curriculum developers tended to classify tasks as involving either low-level or high-level cognitive skills. Low-level tasks would mainly involve the exchange of factual information whereas a high-level task might involve hypothesising or analysing an argument. Other researchers have applied theories of intellectual development so that it is possible to classify tasks in Piagetian terms as either involving concrete or formal operations. More recently, Bennett *et al.* (1984) have made use of information-processing models of learning to define tasks as either incremental, restructuring, enrichment or practice. These researchers argue that by defining tasks in this way teachers can achieve a better match between the needs and abilities of the pupils and the intellectual demands made upon the children by the teacher's choice of activity.

Such an analysis of tasks tends not to consider the effects of self-esteem and self-confidence (both teachers' and pupils') on the content of the activity and the method of instruction. In the previous section, we saw, however, that certain kinds of activities tend to produce a state of anxiety in pupils because of fear of failure. Teachers also experience anxiety, in such situations, partly because of the stress placed on the public accountability of their performance by both authorities and by parents, with the latter group tending to use very crude indicators of success. No analysis of task demand is therefore complete which ignores this social psychological element.

Such an analysis has been offered by the American psychologist, Walter Doyle. Doyle (1983; 1986) classifies tasks according to their degree of ambiguity. The more complex the demands of a task the more likely it is to provoke uncertainty in the minds of the pupils about the outcomes desired by the teacher. When the teacher, for example, sets ten mathematics questions, involving addition and subtraction, little ambiguity is involved. The pupils know exactly what they have to do in order to succeed. However, greater uncertainty is involved if the task is to work as a group to design and make a device which will time exactly two minutes. Pupils will want to know what materials they can use and the teacher's expectations of each individual. When instead of a specific outcome, such as making a timer, pupils (as in Chapter 1) are asked to discuss abstract ideas such as whether the children in the story, *Walkabout*, behaved in a satis-factory manner to the Aborigine who befriended them, an even greater degree of uncertainty will be involved. Children now have no clear idea what an acceptable answer will be. It certainly cannot consist of either yes or no. It is for this reason that the pupils, in their responses to the cartoon pictures, showed a pre-ference for practical tasks rather than those involving discussion.

Doyle (1983) argues that the greater the ambiguity (or uncertainty) surrounding the task the greater the risk involved to the pupils' self-image and hence their self-esteem. This induces fear of failure and leads to adoption of avoidance strategies. Unless, therefore, teachers take active steps to reduce such risks pupils will try to sabotage the teacher's intentions by covert bargaining whereby, only in exchange for a simpler task, will they behave in ways which are deemed more acceptable. Thus Galton (1989) describes an incident whereby the children behaved in an exemplary fashion while they were colouring in the squares of a mathematical crossword (low ambiguity, low risk) but began to disrupt the lesson once they were required to solve the mathematical clues, making it impossible for the teacher to continue the lesson.

Doyle's (1986) conclusion is that the management of the task by the teacher is of vital importance, particularly in cases where teachers set tasks which carry with them a high degree of ambi-guity. In such cases it is important to try to minimise the risks involved to the self-esteem of individual pupils. Jean Wright, intuitively, seems to have recognised this problem and devised strategies for coping with it. Although collectively she adds to the risk element by stressing to pupils the importance that she places upon collaborative activity, she reduces that risk, both for indi-viduals and for individual groups, by refraining from evaluative feedback about their initial attempts at collaboration. When making comments she attributes them to the class in general rather than to one group, or one pupil in particular. She publicly reinforces these tactics by the use of body language, indicating to the pupils, when she joins a group, that she will not comment directly on their activities by placing her hand across her mouth.

Similar principles apply in the case of the jig-saw classroom which was discussed in Chapter 2. Placing pupils in pairs and attaching them to different groups effectively reduces the risk for a particular individual that an idea which he or she offers can be identified as theirs by anyone except the partner in the pair. In the jig-saw method pupils begin discussion in pairs. Thus only one other pupil knows where a particular idea originates when that pair joins other pairs who are all discussing the same issue. Within this first jig-saw grouping, therefore, initial ownership of ideas is further diluted. When the pair subsequently returns to their original group it is possible for them to make a number of contributions to the discussion without disclosing whether they were the originators. If these ideas are taken up by the group they can then disclose ownership thus increasing their prestige among their peers.

This analysis supports the need for the 'two stage' approach to group work which was set out in the previous chapter. It also explains the differences found in the American research literature between the conclusions of Johnson *et al.* (1981) concerning effective group work and those of Slavin (1983b). The Johnsons' studies took place over a two-week period and during this time it can be hypothesised that the pupils' concern was to reduce the risk of failure in the eyes of the teachers or their peers. Over the longer term, as confidence increased, a public demonstration of their contribution to the group's effort, in the form of points awarded to the team's score, becomes more acceptable. Initially, however, as Johnson *et al.* (1981) argue, such competitive structures are likely to prove counterproductive. In her approach to group work Jean seems to have come to similar conclusions to these American researchers.

The discussion so far has tended to minimise the individual differences which undoubtedly exist between pupils and which were reflected in the earlier classification of them as *hardgrinders*, *easy riders* and *attention getters*. Some pupils will already have a reasonable level of self-confidence and even in the initial stages of group work will not be deterred from giving their ideas a public airing. Others, less confident, will be less inclined to have their ideas recognised as their own and be content to take a more passive role in the initial stages. At first these latter pupils may be only too ready to accept suggestions from the teacher. This, in turn, may frustrate the more confident pupils who will see such suggestions as a 'take over'.

Thus, in these settings, the guided discovery approach can offer the worst of both worlds, creating dependency in the less confident pupils and frustration in the more able ones. Jean's approach, although more difficult to sustain, appears to avoid these twin pitfalls. While insisting that all pupils take ownership of their ideas from the start she, nevertheless, minimises the risk that these ideas will be publicly identified as belonging to a particular individual or a particular group in the initial stages. In this way she protects the less confident members of the group until they have succeeded in clarifying the nature of the task to the point where they can risk a public contribution.

GROUP WORK AND CLASSROOM BEHAVIOUR

Another key area in the development of effective strategies for group work would appear to be the style of classroom management adopted by the teacher. The perceptions of the children, based upon their responses to the cartoon pictures, presented a system of negative rewards with the emphasis largely on what we have termed evaluative feedback. Pupils said that the teacher in the cartoon was saying to the group that if they did not finish they would 'have to stay in and miss playtime'. In mathematics, in particular, the emphasis was usually on teachers correcting mistakes and attributing these errors to a lack of concentration on the part of the pupils. Although it would appear, from observations, that this kind of teacher behaviour was not continually in evidence and that there were periods when the class was relaxed and both teachers and pupils were 'not frightened any more', the evidence also suggested that these classroom situations, where teachers took on the role of police-officer and boss figure, loomed very large in the minds of the children. As a result they tended to play safe, particularly in situations where a high degree of task ambiguity was involved. Not getting things wrong in front of the class appeared to be a major preoccupation, so that children would adopt what we have called 'knife edging' strategies or become 'fence straddlers' until teachers provided more directions so that the ambiguity was removed and the pupils knew exactly what was required of them. Teachers tended to use collaborative group work for precisely those occasions when the set task was so complex it required more than one individual to co-operate in reaching a satisfactory answer. Working in groups is therefore the kind of activity which is likely to cause high levels of dependency when strategies for classroom control are of the kind depicted in the cartoon pictures.

However, in the interview with the children, pupils quickly acknowledged that 'Mrs Wright was not like that' and in the observations of her performance on film there was strong support for the pupils' view that Jean Wright was, indeed, different. Four characteristics seemed to identify Jean Wright's style. The first characteristic was the continuity which she attempted to develop between the way in which she controlled classroom behaviour and the way in which she exercised control over the task. Whereas for most teachers the message to children seemed to be 'when it's a question of behaviour – do as I say, but, when it's a question of learning – do as you think', Jean, in both areas, attempted to involve children in decision making. Even in small ways, for example, in moving in and out of the classroom, pupils were trusted to act in ways which were acceptable to the other teachers in contrast to the more controlled style which I adopted (p. 118) when allowing the children to go to the library to change their books. A further example was the different approach of Norma and Jean to lighting candles in the experiment on making a timing device. Norma, it will be remembered, kept the matches and insisted on lighting every pupil's candle whereas Jean placed the matches in a central area and allowed the children to perform the task for themselves (although observing them from a position in neutral space in order to check on the safety of their procedure). In these ways therefore Jean attempted to create an environment which encouraged children to take responsibility not only for the learning but also for the management of that learning.

The second way in which Jean's classroom environment differed from the other teachers' was that she tended to stress the reasons why children engaged in certain tasks so that the pupils 'knew why they were doing things'. Thus in her introduction to group work the importance of co-operation was stressed as was

135

the value of learning through one's mistakes. The children were told repeatedly that the outcome was not the important part of the exercise when making the timing device. Third, when commenting on children's work, at least initially, Jean reduced the amount of evaluative feedback which tended to suggest to pupils what they should do in order to improve their activity. Fourth, she tried, whenever possible, to explore with pupils their feelings when involved either in learning or management situations, creating a degree of empathy by giving accounts of her own emotions when faced with similar circumstances. Thus she told the children what she felt like when she was in a group and no one had taken notice of what she had said. She also identified with the pupils, particularly the girls, in how it felt when one was trying to come to terms with the opposite sex.

Such an approach, in a number of ways, runs contrary to the principles which are generally accepted as providing a useful guide for the management of classrooms. As discussed elsewhere (Galton 1989) teachers are expected to be totally virtuous in their manner of dealing with children. They are expected to be fair at all times so that they treat all children in the same way. They are expected to show a certain degree of aloofness from the children, since it is argued that familiarity will breed contempt. This view is generally confused with showing emotions or feelings of any kind. Indeed the word professional has in certain ways been debased in that instead of being associated, as in Hoyle's (1974) terminology, with a capacity for innovative thinking and action it is more often used in a negative sense to define unprofessional behaviour. Among such instances is an inability to be firm but fair with all pupils and failure to maintain a degree of reserve in one's relationship with children. Teachers such as Jean are thought to 'get away' with a more liberal approach because they are naturally talented and have a personality which allows them to relate easily to pupils. The assumption, therefore, is that the approach which Jean offers is not one that can be generalised to a wide range of classrooms.

However, research into aspects of pupil motivation, carried out in the 1980s, would suggest otherwise so that Jean Wright's classroom practice conforms closely to theory. This research in the United States has focused on children with learning difficulties, particularly a group of pupils who show such dependency upon the teacher that they have been described as demonstrating 'learned helplessness'. Deci and Chandler (1986) point out that previous research into learning difficulties has tended to attribute the cause of the problem either to biological or socio-emotional features characteristic of particular children who therefore require remedial support. Deci and Chandler refer to this as the micro perspective where the treatment requires the identification of the specific problem that the child is having and the teacher then works to ameliorate that problem. Alternatively, a macro approach can be used which establishes general principles of learning and education, principles which apply to all children as well as those with learning difficulties. The research looks for the key features in the classroom environment which encourage children to learn. Central to this latter approach is a view of human motivation which closely matches accepted primary school ideology. For Deci and Chandler

> The human being is an active organism whose activity is vulnerable to certain kinds of forces. By active we mean that the nature of the human being is to experiment, explore, grow and develop. Its nature is to strive for effective interactions with the environment to move from dependence towards autonomy and to construct an ever more elaborate refined and unified internal representation of itself in relation to the world. This unified internal representation plays an increasingly important role in guiding human activity as the human grows older and the activity so guided is energised by biologically braced drives and emotions as well as by innate psychological needs.
>
> (Deci and Chandler 1986: 589)

A number of research studies have focused on the key elements which support this self-determination (Deci and Ryan 1985; Ryan et al. 1985). These researchers make an important distinction between tasks which are inherently interesting to the children and those which, although less interesting, are necessary for the effectiveness of the children's learning. In the earlier chapters, containing various descriptions of classroom activities, there were many examples of such necessary but less interesting activities, as in the fieldnote where the children appeared to lack a 'self-disciplined' approach to scientific activity.

In an interesting paper, Koestner et al. (1984) examined the way in which setting limits on children's behaviour appeared to affect both these intrinsic motivational characteristics and also the element of creativity which a child brought to the task. In their experiment these researchers varied the degree of control on 7 year old children's behaviour when they were engaged in a painting activity. Three kinds of conditions were imposed. For the first, termed *controlling*, pupils were provided with rules which were determined by the teacher. They were told, for example, that they could paint only on a certain size sheet of paper and that they were not to spill paint and that they were to wash their brush and wipe it with a paper towel before changing to a new colour. The second condition, at the other extreme, was a 'no limits' condition where total freedom prevailed. For the third condition children were given clear reasons for the painting rules so that, for example, it was explained that the reason why they should not spill paint on to the backing sheet of paper was that it would subsequently be used as a border for the picture. This approach, the informational limits condition, was very similar to the procedure adopted by Jean. Whenever possible, she explained to the children the reasons why certain tasks were organised in particular ways, for example, when they were required to use biros during the art lesson.

In Koestner *et al.*'s (1984) experiment the teacher asked the pupils to stop painting after ten minutes and then told them that they could either continue or do other activities, including playing with puzzles, which were situated on another table. If a pupil continued painting then this was taken to be a measure of intrinsic motivation. The paintings were also rated by a panel of ten judges on such factors as creativity and expression. Koestner *et al.* (1984) concluded that the controlling style of communication interfered with both the quality of the pupils' performance in creative tasks of this kind and also reduced their intrinsic motivation to pursue the task. Thus, in so far as limits need to be placed on children as part of the socialisation process, it would seem that this should be done in ways which do not require direction on the part of the teacher and the exercise of too firm control. In keeping with previous studies, the *laissez-faire* 'no limits' approach had little to recommend it. It achieved even less satisfactory results than the controlled approach. It is important to realise therefore that what Deci and Ryan (1985) offer as an alternative approach to teacher direction is not, as critics of modern primary practice claim, the equivalent of anarchy.

In summarising the results of the research in this area, Deci and Chandler (1986) provide a list of the major determinants of intrinsic motivation and of pupils' self-determination which are remarkably similar to the very elements identified within the approach used by Jean Wright. These researchers argue, for example, that children need what they term an *optimal challenge*, that is, that the tasks undertaken should be neither too easy nor too difficult. This fits very closely with Jean's approach of placing limits on the complexity of the task. Also important, in Deci's and Chandler's view is the development of an environment that supports the pupils' initiations and allows them to make choices. This environment should not only extend to choices of which cognitive strategy to use but also concern decisions relating to the control of pupils' behaviour. They cite a large number of studies in this area which have shown that pupils in classes of teachers where such an environment existed tended to be intrinsically motivated, perceived themselves to be more competent and developed higher self-esteem than in classrooms where children's behaviour was more directly controlled by the teacher.

Deci and Chandler (1986) place importance on the teacher's use of positive feedback as a way of enhancing a pupil's feeling of competence. They stress that this feedback must be non-controlling so that the teacher, for example, should avoid telling pupils what they 'ought' to do in order to improve. Rather it should be a matter of what Deci and Chandler call 'honest evaluation' which seems very similar to the kinds of discussions which we earlier characterised as 'critical feedback'. Deci and Chandler also stress the need to provide children with a clear understanding of why they are being asked to carry out certain activities. According to Deci and Chandler (1986: 591) telling children that they are doing things for their own good is not a rationale but a way of controlling their behaviour. On the other hand telling pupils that 'it is important for me to have our classroom looking nice and I would like you to help me do that' is a more honest rationale for asking children to clear up the mess.

Deci and Chandler (1986) also stress the value of teachers and pupils acknowledging each other's feelings. In a direct parallel to the incident in Jean's class (p. 114) Deci and Chandler argue that while 'it is not OK for the boy to hit his friend when he is angry' it may be 'OK for him to feel angry'. They suggest that a comment like 'I see that you are angry but it is not OK for you to hit him'

139

would help the pupil integrate what he is feeling with what he is being asked to do (Deci and Chandler 1986: 591). This example provides a carbon copy of the strategy used by Jean in the incident where a boy hit a girl. In exactly the same way my experience with the child, who was frightened to touch the soil because of the creatures in it (p. 120), conveyed a similar message that while I wanted her to put her fingers in the soil I understood why she found it difficult to do so.

Elsewhere Galton (1989) has written extensively of the ways in which teachers can develop a non-controlling classroom environment which corresponds closely to the one recommended by Deci and Chandler (1986). The suggested approach, developed while observing and working alongside Jean Wright, corresponds closely to that set out in Thomas Gordon's (1974) programme of *Teacher Effectiveness Training* and also to the control theories of Glasser (1986). Glasser argues that many problems of classroom control, which teachers experience, are owned by them and not by the pupils. It is, for example, often teachers' self-image, in the eyes of their colleagues, which is at stake when children are noisy, untidy or appear to lack concentration. Yet as teachers we persistently treat such problems as if they are a deficiency in the child so that we accuse them of being 'noisy', 'untidy', or of 'not paying attention' as in the cartoon pictures. Gordon (1974) recommends that we should seek to limit sending pupils these accusatory 'you' messages and instead, as Deci and Chandler (1986) advocate, provide honest evaluations whereby we explain, through the use of 'I' messages, the legitimate reason why it is necessary to have a measure of order and quiet within the classroom. Instead of telling the pupils that 'You are too noisy' the teacher informs the class that 'The noise level has risen' and 'I find it difficult to listen to what children are telling me'. Gordon (1974) goes further and suggests that the teacher then explains how this noise affects her by telling the pupils she is concerned lest in this situation she is missing something important which a pupil is trying to tell her.

All these approaches recognise that for effective learning to take place, including learning within groups, children require that limits are set and clear structures for operating within these limits established. The important question, however, as Gordon (1974) argues is not whether there is a need for such structures but how these structures should be determined. The research reviewed by Deci and Chandler (1986) seems to suggest that when tasks involve a high level of ambiguity, this structure should not be imposed by the teacher but should, as far as possible, be negotiated with the pupils. In the process teachers need to provide clear reasons why such procedures are necessary. Kutnick (1990) is correct, when advocating ways of developing pupil autonomy, to point out that in the eyes of the pupils, teachers have power in the classroom by virtue of their status, but his statement needs qualification. It is possible for this power to be accepted by pupils without the teacher having to impose a set of rules governing the classroom environment.

Thus the only alternative open to teachers is not to abandon their authority and become the 'pupil's friend' and collaborator in the manner often attributed to 'progressive' educators. Jean Wright seems to have realised that the dichotomy proposed by such an analysis is a false one. She has taken a position where, although her authority is recognised by the pupils in her class, she still seeks to minimise the occasions when she uses it unilaterally. When forced to impose her authority she still makes it clear to the children that she understands the feeling which led to their behaviour. Whenever possible she explains clearly the reasons for certain decisions and invites children to comment on her solutions to problems. In her approach she can draw support from the most recent evidence on children's intrinsic motivation and on managing environments which achieve satisfactory outcomes on complex tasks demanding the use of the pupils' creative imagination.

TEACHING DILEMMAS AND THE IMPLEMENTATION OF COLLABORATIVE GROUP WORK

The above discussion should not be interpreted as offering a straightforward selection of teaching strategies which it is possible to implement consistently from lesson to lesson. These recommendations are not offered as 'tips for teaching' but are rather a set of principles which can be applied to the art of teaching in the manner suggested by Gage (1985). This scientific approach recognises that to apply such principles in a given classroom context will always be problematic. The factors which determine the behaviour, motivation, cognitive state of the pupils at the start of the lesson will vary from occasion to occasion. As observed elsewhere (Galton 1990) too much emphasis in training teachers is based upon the acquisition of what might be termed 'entry strategies'. Students are told repeatedly that if only they had not done certain things or behaved in certain ways then they would have avoided the consequences which led to ineffective teaching. The study of expert teachers (Berliner 1987) suggests, however, that their effectiveness depends largely on the use of what might be termed 'exiting' strategies. Experts – having realised, after the event has begun, that a particular teaching approach will lead to unwelcome consequences – are able to call upon a repertoire of strategies designed to allow them to escape from the situation with dignity and with the appearance that all has proceeded according to plan. In any given lesson, therefore, teachers are continually presented with what Berlak and Berlak (1981) call teaching dilemmas for which they have to work out and select suitable 'exiting' strategies.

In the matter of group work we can identify three key areas where such dilemmas are likely to occur. The first concerns the need to provide a clear rationale for each activity and the manner in which the teacher then evaluates subsequent work against these criteria. The use of collaborative group work, as we have seen from Chapter 1, can be readily justified on a number of grounds, including the improvement of understanding among slow learners, the development of teaching skills among their peers and the general development of social cohesion and collaboration within a group of children. At any one point in time during a lesson the teacher may have all of these objectives in mind having explained these purposes clearly to the class. However, when intervening within a particular group in order to provide feedback, a teacher will naturally tend to base the judgement on some more specific criteria appropriate to the particular situation. Thus some children may be praised because they have shown social responsibility in that they have reduced the amount of disruptive behaviour. Praise might be withheld from another group because they have not produced a sufficiently coherent outcome. Teachers when making such judgements do so on the basis of their individual knowledge of children, which other members of the class or of other groups, may not share.

From the pupils' point of view, however, the situation may be one of confusion. For children to understand the teacher's evaluation they must be party to the criteria on which the particular judgement is based. It is then necessary for the teacher to go beyond an explanation of the general purposes of group work towards the creation of a set of clear criteria against which pupils can judge their own performance prior to any evaluation by the teacher. Thus when dealing with social relationships in groups pupils should consider a range of roles, in addition to that of leadership, including helping to identify goals, summarising viewpoints, acting as 'willing followers' (who carry out tedious tasks such as tidying up and generally keeping things going) helping to resolve disputes and focusing the discussion when it wanders from the point. In Chapter 7, which examines monitoring and evaluation of group work, we shall look at ways in which such criteria can be established.

The second dilemma facing teachers concerns their attempt to give pupils individual ownership of their ideas while at the same time minimising any sense of personal failure. In most situations teachers will have an understanding of the individual child's capability, based upon past experience, and will, therefore, attempt to set them realistic goals. As a result some children will be rewarded for doing less amounts of work than others because it is the teacher's judgement that this accords with their capabilities. A teacher is naturally reluctant to make public these considerations lest the slower learning pupil would be hurt by exposure to this appraisal. On the other hand other children who see a pupil being rewarded for a limited outcome may consider their own treatment unfair unless they understand the rationale behind the teacher's judgements. An approach is required where the criteria are negotiated prior to the setting of the task and where the pupil has a part in the subsequent evaluation of his or her contribution to the group.

Third, there will exist many difficulties in creating a classroom environment where there is continuity between the methods used to control both behaviour and learning in the manner suggested by Deci and Chandler (1986). Teachers who successfully negotiate the rules of classroom behaviour with the class enjoy a major advantage over other colleagues in that when the pupils do not obey these rules it is no longer a personal reflection on the teacher's authority. However, there will be instances where teachers are required to use their power directly to control pupils' behaviour, particularly in cases where a pupil endangers others or where the individuals concerned do not appear to respond to this kind of treatment. On other occasions, as Galton

(1989) describes, the stress of the situation will lead the teacher to resort to the more secure and familiar situation of acting as police-officer.

It is important, however, to realise that such situations can be retrieved by the application of the principles set out in the previous chapters. As Gordon (1974) observes it is always possible for teachers to apologise to the class after an excessive display of one's authority choosing the next suitable occasion to explain the circumstances and the feelings which led to the particular action. Galton (1989) describes such a situation, where in the subsequent discussion pupils responded, in most moving terms, by explaining the problems they experienced, in terms of their self-esteem, when they were asked to read aloud with expression. Out of such discussions can come a developing understanding between the teacher and the pupil which produces a classroom environment, as in Jean's class, which facilitates challenging, highly ambiguous and risk-taking activities such as those which involve collaboration in groups.

The theories discussed in this chapter confirm the effectiveness of the strategies for facilitating group work, intuitively developed by teachers such as Jean Wright. These strategies provide children with a clear rationale for working in groups and direct training in the skills required to participate in them effectively. At the initial stage, tasks which carry as little ambiguity as possible are preferable and the demands made upon the pupils should be broken down into small steps that reduce the potential challenge and guarantee a reasonable level of success for a majority of pupils involved.

Finally the classroom ethos in which collaboration can flourish is one where there is a consistency in the way in which teachers deal with issues related to classroom management and with matters relating to learning. Ways of working *with* groups as well as ways of learning *in* groups need to be the subject of negotiation between the teacher and the pupils. A powerful element in this negotiation process is the development of a shared understanding about the feelings generated by the requirement to collaborate with one's peers and an awareness that these feelings are responsible for certain kinds of behaviour when working in group settings.

7

BEGINNING AND MAINTAINING GROUP WORK

STARTING GROUP WORK

Having established in the previous chapters the strategies which are required in order to promote effective collaboration in the primary classroom we now turn to look at some of the ways in which teachers who took part in the ORACLE II project initiated and helped to sustain these group activities. Although, as we have seen, teachers find it difficult to articulate the reasons why they choose to work in certain ways rather than in others they, nevertheless, have a perspective concerning the way in which children learn and this affects the way in which they structure their teaching. However, whereas a psychologist, who had a particular view of learning, might plan a lesson by translating this view into a series of pre-specified operationally defined objectives with both the content of the lesson and the method of instruction chosen to match these prescribed goals, teachers generally work from the opposite direction and select the content and the method to fit the context in which the teaching has to take place. Evidence to support this assertion comes from Calderhead (1984) who in his study of teacher decision making found that,

> Teachers faced with a variety of factors such as pupils with certain knowledge, abilities and interests, the availability of particular text books and materials, the syllabus, the timetable, the expectations of headteachers and others and their own knowledge of previous teaching encounters have to solve the problem of how to structure the time and experience of the pupils in the classroom. Teachers, it seems, adopt a much more pragmatic approach than that prescribed for curriculum design. Rather than start with a

conception of what is to be achieved and deduce which classroom activities would therefore be ideal, teachers start with a conception of the working context of what is possible.
(Calderhead 1984: 74)

This approach to curriculum planning has been termed pragmatic scepticism by Doyle and Ponder (1977) who argue that teachers are chiefly concerned to investigate a problem with the intention of achieving a workable solution which will solve the difficulties which they are facing at the particular time in the classroom. Teachers try to recall what it is they know works in the classroom and what therefore is possible in a given context. In any new situation a teacher will weigh the anticipated benefits which result in a particular course of action, what Doyle and Ponder (1977) call the practicality ethic. This practicality ethic is usually tested against three criteria before it is adopted. The first of these, *instrumentality*, requires teachers to decide whether or not the innovation can be implemented in the classroom without any modification. The second criterion, *congruence*, requires the teacher to decide whether the curriculum innovation can be accommodated within the teacher's existing classroom style or whether they need to modify their behaviour. The third criterion, *cost*, takes into account the expenditure of effort, time and other resources that the teacher needs to spend to implement the innovation successfully. This cost is then set against the innovations perceived value as a tool for learning. In each teaching situation the teacher, albeit unconsciously, weighs the anticipated benefits against these criteria and only introduces an activity if these limitations are outweighed significantly by what the pupil is expected to learn or the interest which it is thought the activity will generate. Since most of the tasks, described in the next section, were the result of a considerable amount of teacher effort and were recommended as part of the in-service courses, which the teachers taking part in the ORACLE II project designed for their colleagues, we may infer that they conform to this practicality ethic.

In creating these tasks the participating teachers first engaged in considerable debate about the best way to get started when seeking to develop group work in the classroom. The central issue of this debate can be exemplified by a recorded discussion between several teachers which took place during one of the in-service day planning sessions.

Ann   Unless the organisation is sorted out you can't go
         forward.
Peter   In my case I felt it would be an idea to train the children
         in working in groups at the start. Whereas I think
         Graham's plan was to choose ongoing topics and intro-
         duce the groups as an integral part of the topic. I was
         choosing topics to teach the skills of group work and I
         am only now integrating this into ongoing topic work.
Graham   I was able to teach mine the skills of group work before
         they became my class.
David   Are you suggesting that firstly you deliberately teach
         certain skills which you think are appropriate to group
         work?
Sheila   What we want are ways into group work not a recipe.

This fragment of discussion illustrates the existence of differences
in approach. One group of teachers argued that children should
first be provided with some specific skills training before they
could be expected to operate in groups. This view was, however,
not adopted by the majority, although it was the one which
appeared to ensure success for Jean Wright and which was
supported by the theory developed in Chapter 6. Other teachers
in the ORACLE II project, however, decided that they would
rather devise tasks which had the required skills of group work
embedded in them. In this way pupils' interest would be best
served if the tasks were designed to lead students implicitly to the
skills rather than to teach those skills explicitly. The absence or
presence of the required skills were then identified as part of the
concluding evaluation, usually by replaying the audio tape of the
discussions.

Among the tasks chosen for this purpose were the following.

1 A group of two or three children was provided with an assort-
   ment of sticky paper shapes (squares, circles, triangles, etc.) and
   another larger piece of sugar paper. The task for the group of
   children was to create an animal or a creature from the sticky
   shapes, the composition of which had to suit the shape of the
   background sugar paper. The group had to decide together on
   a name for their creation. The teacher's role was to decide
   whether or not the group had used up all the shapes provided
   and whether or not it was possible to recognise and identify the
   animal which they had created. (reception/infants)

2 A box of varied colours and lengths of ribbon was given to three children. The task for the group was to display the ribbons on a flat surface in order of length, starting with the shortest and finishing with the longest. (infants)

3 Four or five children are asked to cut out people from magazines and arrange them on a single sheet of sugar paper to form a queue at the bus stop. The children have to discuss who is at the front of the queue and whether the people are alone or if there are too many men, women or children. The group decides who is to draw the bus stop and where the bus is going. Teacher intervention is necessary to put these questions but not to interrupt further. The conversation is taped and the children then listen to it later. (6+)

4 A group of children is given four circles of wallpaper, each of a different pattern and about 20 cm in diameter. The circles are marked into quarters and the children have to cut these out and then rearrange the circles on a large background sheet so that the pattern in each circle is unique. This task is best given to groups of two children but can be extended to groups of four by giving eight circles of different patterns marked into eighths. (6+)

5 A page from a comic strip is cut into separate compartments and the group is asked to place them in the right order. Each comic piece is mounted on to paper which is just big enough to leave a narrow border so that the children can 'jig-saw' them back together. If a more difficult task is required then one of the squares can be held back and children are asked to work out where the gap is. (7+)

6 Five or six children are provided with a selection of objects which they can handle such as a shoe, teapot, bottle, glove, etc. They are then asked to discuss the following. 'If you shrank down to the size of a pin, which object would make the best home for you and why? How would you improve the object to make it a more comfortable home?' (7+)

All these tasks were devised for work with children in the 4–7 year age range on the assumption that group work cannot be started too early and the skills need to be built up over the whole primary period. They are, according to our definition, low-risk activities and are likely to lead mainly to practical rather than abstract conversations. Reasonable levels of collaboration can therefore be achieved by embedding skills within these simple tasks and then drawing attention to the successful practice during the subsequent evaluation. The evidence suggests that for more complex tasks, such as the following which were proposed for junior aged pupils, a more structured approach is necessary if the discussion is to involve all the pupils.

7 The teacher divided the class into groups of four. The children had to design an experiment which was fair, to show the best conditions for growing some broad beans. (10+)
8 The teacher set the children to work in groups of five and gave each group a worksheet involving a cloze procedure exercise. (10+)
9 The teacher allowed the children to form their own groups of six. Their task is to prepare a list of school rules which they would like to see implemented when they move to their new school building. (9+)

Thus, for topic 7, where children carried out an experiment, under controlled conditions, to find the best way of growing beans, there was considerable collaboration on the routine matters of organising the planting and maintaining the seeds by creating a roster for watering and measuring their growth. When working out the exact conditions to carry out the fair testing, however, considerable teacher input seemed to be required.

Pupil	Miss Newton, when we took it out yesterday it only had little tiny brown marks and there was brown and red . . .
Teacher	Have you noticed the inside of the bean?
Pupil	Yes, Miss. There are big brown patches there. You either get brown patches, I suppose, or black. It's probably food, Miss.
Teacher	On looking back on what we have been talking about this morning, how could you improve your experiments? What's one conclusion you have come to already?
Pupil	Measure more accurately.
Teacher	What about the angle of the bean?
Pupil	You put them in the same way?
Another pupil	You must try to find out which way they go up.

Teacher	How can you tell? How could you prove it so that you planted them all the right way up?
Pupil	We could plant two beans. You could put one in one way and the other with another and see which goes better and remember which one we put in which way.
Teacher	Let's not think about these beans in the soil at first. Let's think about how we have just started when we soaked the beans. What happened to them when we soaked them? What did they start to do?
Pupil	They went sort of pappy and bigger.
Teacher	What did they start to do? What special word did we start talking about?
Pupil	Germinate.
Teacher	Yes. They started to germinate. So think about how you could make sure that all these went in the right way.
Pupil	We could mmmm ...
Teacher	Thinking about when we soaked the beans they started to germinate.
Pupil	I know, let the root grow.
Teacher	That's right. So let the root grow for a little so that you can see what?
Pupil	Which way you put it in.
Teacher	Which way. OK. That's good and then that's one way you can improve that experiment. That's smashing. Don't forget that one and what I will do now is to leave you to discover other ways of improving this because there are other ways.

This extract provides a classic illustration of the problem that can arise with the guided discovery approach where the teacher, Miss Newton, is forced to offer more and more clues so that the exercise becomes, in effect, one where the children have to guess what is in the teacher's mind. While it could be argued that the main problem was that the idea of fair testing was too difficult for the children to deal with independently, the examples in Chapters 4 and 5 suggest that greater progress might have been made if the complexity of the task had been reduced and clearer directions had been provided about how children were to conduct the exchanges within the groups. As with Norma, who also favoured the guided discovery approach, there is evidence in later transcripts that the children in Miss Newton's class achieve more independence and this comes about as part of the evaluation of the lesson on growing beans. For this particular exercise on growing beans each group was required to make an edited tape of their discussion in which they picked out what they perceived to be the important highlights. These edited tapes were then played back to the whole class and discussed. Some of the taped extracts showed, for example, that only one pupil in the group had been responsible for most of the key ideas and this issue was taken up by Miss Newton who then asked why none of the other pupils contributed. In this way pupils in her class began to understand more clearly that in such discussions the teacher's expectation was that more than one child would contribute to the ideas.

In other cases, without the lack of a clear understanding about the purposes of group work, the task seemed to present enormous difficulties for the pupils, as with Topic 8 where children were asked to tackle a cloze procedure exercise to do with cures for snoring (Walker 1979). The group of pupils was given a single worksheet containing the following paragraph and told to fill in the ten missing words.

> One cure is to sleep with several pillows. This..(1).. the head when asleep and helps to keep the..(2).. closed. Or a small pillow can be placed under..(3).. nape of the neck. If all these remedies fail..(4).. is a lot to be said for an old..(5).. cure. This is to sew hard objects into the..(6).. of the pyjamas. A stone or a hairbrush is..(7).. sewn in. Should the sleeper turn on his..(8).. while sleeping the stone or the brush will..(9).. He is then able to turn on his side..(10)..

The tape recording of the ensuing discussion was as follows.

Pupil 1   What's number 6?
Pupil 2   Back.
Pupil 3   Pack.
Pupil 1   Pack? Back.
Pupil 3   How do you know?
Pupil 1   Cure, this is to sew hard objects into their pack. No it's not.
Pupil 2   Back not pack.
Pupil 4   Bag.
Pupil 2   Back.
Pupil 1   Come on, put back down. That's you showing off isn't it?

Pupil 2   That's head. Number 8 is head. Should the sleeper turn on his head while sleeping?

Pupil 5   Right, what are we on to now?

Pupil 3   I'm just going through them. The stone or brush will soon wake up.

Pupil 5   I think 9 is up, woke up.

Pupil 2   That's wrong. He's put head. The head.

Pupil 3   That's what you said.

Pupil 2   It's not the head.

Pupil 3   You said head.

Pupil 2   It can't be. This meant the head. It's not head. Look it doesn't make sense.

Pupil 4   Rub it out. It's meant. This meant the head.

Pupil 1   Allright, if it is wrong it is your fault.

Pupil 4   Good.

Pupil 1   The eyes.

Pupil 2   The eyes closed or a small . . . It doesn't make sense.

Pupil 3   I'll write it but it is your fault if we get it wrong.

Pupil 1   Come on. How much have you got to do?

Pupil 4   We've only got two more.

Pupil 1   We've got 4, 6 and 7.

Pupil 3   Two more. Let's do 7. Hairbrush is something sewn in.

Pupil 2   I don't get it.

Pupil 1   We're stuck, Mrs Moody.

Pupil 2   Shut up we've got to get on with it.

While it might be argued that part of the reason for the behaviour of the children was that they were uninterested in the task (hence their desire to finish it as quickly as possible) there was also clear evidence that the children were reluctant to accept ownership of the solution. Instead they accepted, without too much detailed scrutiny, the suggestion put forward by one of the pupils, providing that pupil accepted total responsibility for the result. As the research findings suggest such tasks contain too many demands on the pupils and unless they are broken down into smaller elements they are likely to result in the kind of disorganised discussion portrayed in the above extract. Through this and other experiences teachers in ORACLE II were able to draw up a checklist which enabled them to decide whether a given task might prove suitable for groups of children who were relatively inexperienced in working together collaboratively. This list consisted of the following ten questions.

Does the task:

1 Provide each child with an opportunity to be physically involved (e.g. handling apparatus).
2 Give an opportunity for each child to take part actively (e.g. in making a verbal contribution).
3 Involve only skills of which the children already have some understanding.
4 Have a definite objective so that the children know when they have finished.
5 Require the children to work in a way that it would be difficult for one child to complete the activity alone.
6 Offer a structure so that there is a definite logical progression of stages.
7 Have a clearly laid out set of instructions.
8 Have the appropriate equipment and resources readily to hand.
9 Lend itself to being done in a normal classroom situation (time, space and noise).
10 Allow for the minimal need of teacher support or intervention initially.

MONITORING AND MAINTAINING GROUP WORK

One of the most difficult tasks undertaken during the ORACLE II project was to develop procedures which allowed the teachers to monitor and maintain group work while it was taking place. The matter was discussed at a number of workshop sessions. At first little progress was made in actually recording what was going on in classrooms, partly because the presence of the teacher in the group tended to disturb the situation. In an attempt to provide more stimulus materials for future discussion teachers were asked to set small tasks for a group of children in a classroom and to try to record what it was they observed. In one example the teacher gave a group of children a card with the title of a story, 'the buried gun'. The children were told that there was a beautiful rusty gun and it was to be found buried in a garden. The card told the pupils a little about it and the teacher then gave the children the following instructions.

153

I want you to write down a list of chapter headings and I want you to try and order them so that they work from perhaps a story or an account right through to the end. And then I want you to write the story, just the headings. You remember that you have seen chapter headings before, haven't you.

The following is part of the conversation between the children.

First girl	Read the card out, Tim.
First boy	This rusty gun was dug up in a garden about two years ago. It was half a meter down in the soil and was in exactly the same condition as you see it now.
First girl	We have got to write a story about it.
Second girl	No, just the headings.
First boy	What is going to be the first chapter heading then?
First girl	Like an introduction theme.
First boy	Rachael, you write it down.
Second girl	The first chapter could be where it was found.
First girl	Then what happened after he found the gun.
First boy	It could have come from Paris, or somewhere.
Second boy	It could be a mystery.
First boy	Yes, the mystery of the gun.
Second boy	Second.
First boy	No, first.
Second girl	Yes, finding the gun first and the mystery of the gun second.
First girl	Don't put the numbers down just yet. Just pick the ideas and then we can swop them about after.
Same girl	We'll have a vote on it.
First boy	The mystery of the gun. No. We've got that.
Second girl	Put down mysterious happenings.
First boy	Where was it found?
First girl	It doesn't matter.
Second boy	The owner of the gun.
Second girl	Yes and the gun goes missing.
Second boy	It could be my grandad's or something.
Second girl	How many chapters are we meant to have.
First boy	Don't know.
Second boy	I suppose about seven.
First girl	As many as you can get.
Second girl	How many have we got so far? Five.

First girl	Right. Let's put them in order. Write them down.
First boy	Finding the gun first.
Second boy	Second?
All together	The owner.
First boy	Third, the mystery of the gun.
First girl	No, I think the second one will be the mystery because the owner would be wondering where it is and that.
First boy	Yes. The mystery is number two.
Teacher	Have you got some titles? Have you got some headings?
All pupils	Yes.

The above discussion contains a number of interesting elements. The two girls in particular play an important role in helping to sustain the discussion making crucial interventions at times when the group appears to become bogged down. Thus the first girl makes the suggestion that they should not put the numbers down but just get the ideas first and the second girl suggests, when later they cannot agree on the order, that they should vote and take the majority view. Again, further on in the transcript, the second girl makes an important intervention when changing the order of the headings so that the mystery of the gun is placed before the discovery by the owner that the gun is missing.

The teacher's account of these exchanges, based largely on her impressions, was carried out under conditions where the other children in the class were supervised by a researcher from the project so that, in a sense, it was an artificial situation. The teacher's account read as follows:

Immediately I left one boy (Tim) picked up the card and began to read it aloud to the group. The straightforward nomination of Rachael as the writer took place with no argument at this decision and this appeared to set the tone for the activity.

Although it was obvious that the children were on their best behaviour in this somewhat artificial situation where I was observing them continually it was also apparent that most of the group knew what was expected of them. The four contributed well to get things going. They began by planning the story outline, discussing possible developments, working out background details concerning

155

the finding of the gun and considered factors that might have caused its loss and a possible identity of the owner. They even dealt with the suggestion that the gun might have magical properties.

The tone of the discussion was reasonably mature. The language exchange was well expressed, respect was shown for each other's contributions, consideration was given to the sequential development and the length of the story. Tim and Elaine emerged as the co-ordinators of the discussion, Tim initiating new aspects and Elaine rounding up each sequence to a conclusion. Voting was suggested as a possibility for resolving an area of dispute over the story element.

Four of the group showed considerable imagination in their contribution and it became noticeable that two of the group, Leigh and Louise, were very quiet and placid and that the others made no direct attempt to involve these two. By the time I rejoined the group the list of seven chapter headings had been agreed. It was then discussed with the children and at this stage Leigh and Louise did become involved. After the experience had been completed the group were asked to fill in a self-evaluation questionnaire of their evaluations of their own level of participation agreed with those of the teacher observer. All, except Leigh, thought the group had no leader. They all suggested that they could not have done better on their own. One girl felt that there had not been enough time to complete the project while another felt that they could have done better if they had not been distracted by the surroundings. My general conclusion was that the children had concentrated very well and produced a positive outcome.'

The teachers' impressionistic account picked out a number of key features which can also be verified from the detailed transcript, for example, the role of Tim in initiating new aspects and Elaine's capacity to bring a discussion to a conclusion. However, most teachers expressed doubts as to whether they could have picked up as much detail if they had not been free to concentrate on a single group. Accordingly a number of more sophisticated techniques was attempted involving both audio and video tape. The general view was that video tape created a somewhat artificial situation albeit that the uses reported took place before the availability of small hand-held cameras. Even with these instruments, however, the recording of dialogue proved problematic. Teachers were divided about using a portable video camera. While the static camera gives a limited picture, when the person recording moves around it tends to disturb the group and the pictures are likely to be biased unless an agreed procedure has been developed beforehand. In such situations, it also requires a second person to be present. While, therefore, a video tape gives a very detailed permanent pictorial and sound record which can be analysed at leisure it came as something of a surprise that the teachers did not think it was superior to the simpler audio record. Use of a tape recorder, particularly one which had a built-in microphone and so provided a permanent record of the conversations, was favoured and teachers usually had little difficulty in picking out the individual children with whom they were familiar. There were, however, disadvantages when attempting to discuss the transcript with other teachers who were not familiar with the content. In such cases it was found useful to make a permanent pictorial record using a 35 mm instamatic camera with a built-in flash. Such a pictorial record also offered advantages when discussing the group activity with the children subsequently. The greatest problem, however, remained the time it took to make a permanent record for analysis. This disadvantage was partly overcome by some teachers who developed the technique of editing the initial transcript on to a second tape so that only key features were then transcribed.

Systematic observation was used by many teachers at the initial stage as a way of identifying mainly quantitative collaboration such as which pupils were participating in discussion or which groups sustained their interactions across several time intervals. However, attempts to include a measure of qualitative performance produced a very complex category system which was too difficult for teachers to use under normal classroom conditions. Nevertheless the exercise in itself was found to be a valuable one because in the process of creating these categories, setting up specific structured teaching activities and then attempting to classify the behaviours, teachers came to a set of agreed definitions by which they were more confident that when talking about group work they did so in terms of a common language. Thus general talk about leadership qualities was gradually refined into sub-categories dealing with authority and negotiation roles.

As a first step, therefore, the teachers developed for themselves simple monitoring checklists from which they sought to gain information via the 'spirit level method' describing the broad patterns of involvement. In addition, teachers also noted briefly the methods of recording used by children in particular activities and some of the various roles undertaken by the pupils during the group sessions. After several sessions with this monitoring approach the ORACLE II teachers decided that these data gathering approaches were not providing them with the detailed information which they required in order to evaluate the success of the activity. Accordingly the research team was asked to help develop a more comprehensive systematic category system which could then be used to provide the information that they required.

ANALYSING PUPIL DISCUSSION

The category system which was developed in the effective group work study was derived from tape recorded discussion sessions. The difficulties in this approach have been well documented. Bellack *et al.* (1966), for example, have written on the difficulty of developing a category system to monitor classroom language and a more recent review of the problems (Edwards and Westgate, 1987) indicates that two decades later many of these problems remain. Tann's (1981) study, which was connected with the initial ORACLE research, also showed how difficult it was to construct a system which was reliable, inclusive and meaningful. Among the difficulties in developing a category system to monitor classroom talk is that the most accessible, isolatable utterances are not necessarily the most important (Barnes and Todd 1977). In many instances it is just as important for an understanding of what is happening to have a record of those utterances which have their meaning embedded in much earlier parts of the discussion or in the tone of an utterance or in some associated non-linguistic behaviour. The category system developed for the teachers in the ORACLE II group work project therefore attempted to balance the need for an explicit framework with the desirability of including as many possible contextual factors that were thought to influence discussions in groups. Accordingly no division was made between the content and the social interactions as was the case in earlier systems such as Bales and Cohen (1979) and

Sinclair and Coulthard (1975). Analysis of the initial transcripts seems to indicate that most utterances could be categorised by the effect that they had on the discussion: whether they promoted it, generated further ideas or caused the discussion to falter or change direction. Successful group discussion appeared to go through certain stages, an orientation stage, a development stage and a concluding stage. There was in the orientation phase a certain amount of 'stage setting' where agreements were made either explicitly or implicitly about the ways to proceed. The second phase, the development stage, concentrated on the issues at hand and at the third stage, the concluding phase, agreements were reached about the issue or there were agreements to differ over outcomes.

It also became apparent that the behaviour of pupils while engaging in these different stages of discussion could be distinguished by the particular roles that they played in the process. Pupils were described either as leaders, active participants, willing followers or saboteurs. These broad categories could be further divided into a number of specific components. For example the key characteristic of pupils displaying a *leader* role was the dominant behaviour. In this area a pupil might organise the task by defining the problem, identifying the goal or sub-goal and setting targets. He or she might allocate the work between students, decide who did what and then summarise the discussion by rephrasing contributions and pulling together the different view points and interpretations and finally offer solutions or press for conclusions for the matter under discussion. These essentially were authoritative roles but leaders might also operate through negotiation as *active participants* who were characterised by their ability to stimulate this negotiating behaviour in the other members of the group. Such pupils were seen to initiate ideas and suggestions, raise questions and challenge statements and assertions in ways that enabled the discussion to move forward. They assessed the progress of groups as they clarified ideas and sought to gain the agreement on discussions that were taking place.

Willing followers were characterised by good-natured support of the discussion. Often the pupil in this role acted as a gatekeeper who might, for example, suggest turn taking so that momentum was maintained and every member of the group was able to contribute. Such students would be encouraging and conciliatory when different responses were given by several group members and often they relieved the tension in the group through a joke. At times such pupils would show altruistic behaviour by taking on unpopular tasks or conceding an advantage to other students.

The final group of students was termed *saboteurs* although in the final version of the schedule this term was dropped because it was considered too pejorative and the behaviours described were simply classified as non-cooperative. The behaviour of this group was characterised by negative or destructive actions. For example, such pupils would attack or reject outright all suggestions made by other pupils. They often held back progress in the group by raising problems or stressing difficulties. At times such students might withdraw from the group interaction and refuse to participate or exhibit destructive behaviour which then prevented other group members from continuing with the task. The full schedule is presented in Figure 7.1.

By way of illustration the following two short extracts provide examples of the coding system. In both cases children in two parallel classes aged 9+ were engaged in discussing a set of school rules made up of the following

No talking allowed in schools.
Children must wear school uniform.
No running in the corridors.
All children must leave school at 3.30 p.m.
Children must eat all their dinner.
All parents must bring their children into the classroom in the morning.

First boy	Right, all children must leave school at 3.30 p.m. (Cat 1)
First girl	I think that's quite a good rule because . . . (Cat 5)
Second girl	It's OK if you are having an activity then it is OK to stay. But otherwise you would be left wandering about. (Cat 6)
First girl	Your parents might be wondering where you are. (Cat 7)
First boy	After school, the cleaners might leave the floor saturated and you might have slippery shoes on and you might slip. (Cat 5)
First girl	Yes, you might suddenly go flying. (Cat 7)
Second girl	If the children hang about at school then you might get into trouble, you know. (Cat 5)

AUTHORITY ROLES: leadership behaviours
1 ORGANISES task – defines goal, sets targets, etc.
2 ALLOCATES work
3 SUMMARISES – pulls together, interprets
4 OFFERS SOLUTIONS – presses for conclusion

NEGOTIATING ROLES: supportive behaviours
5 INITIATES ideas, suggestions
6 QUESTIONS – CHALLENGES – keeps things going
7 CO-ORDINATES ideas
8 SUMMARISES – analyses ideas for clarification
9 ASSESSES progress
10 TRIES to get AGREEMENT – avoids stalemate
11 EVALUATES – makes a judgement about value of solution/idea
12 ENCOURAGES – asks, involves others

SUPPORTIVE ROLES: maintenance behaviours
13 FOLLOWS – listens to others, makes sympathetic utterances
14 GATEKEEPS – follows correct procedures, keeps things going
15 ALTRUISTIC behaviour – takes on unpopular task, concedes advantage
16 CONCILIATES – irons out differences, minimises disagreements
17 RELIEVES tension – jokes, etc.
18 RESIGNATION
19 ACCEPTS prevailing situation – willingly goes along with decisions

NON-COOPERATIVE ROLES: non-functional behaviours
20 AGGRESSION – attacks or rejects all suggestions outright, reacts aggressively
21 BLOCKING – blocks progress by raising problems/difficulties, reacts negatively
22 SELF-CONFESSING
23 SEEKS SYMPATHY
24 SPECIAL PLEADING
25 HORSEPLAY – fools around in a disruptive way
26 WITHDRAWAL – refuses to participate

Figure 7.1 Classification of group process

Here, in the main, the children stick to the point of the discussion and the exchanges are mainly leading or supporting whereas in another group, discussing the name rule, the transcript was as follows:

First boy	All children should leave school at 3.30 p.m. (Cat 1)
First girl	No. (Cat 6)
Second girl	Put your hand up if you think you should leave. (Cat 4)
First girl	If you go on a trip with the school you won't be back at 3.30 p.m. then. (Cat 5)
Third boy	At my mum's work you get ... (Cat 21)
First girl	Who wants to know about your mum's work? The tape don't! (Cat 20)
Third boy	Also, there isn't enough good books in the school. (Cat 21)
First girl	They are all old books. (Cat 19)
First boy	I mean, when you have reading sessions it takes you about an hour in a reading session to pick a book from our class. (Cat 21)
Third girl	I know. (Cat 12)
First boy	When you play snowballs though, it hurts. When it goes in your eyes and that. (Cat 21)
Third girl	I don't think it's fair on girls having to use the girls' toilets in the winter. (Cat 5)
Second girl	I don't think you should be allowed to bring toy cars into school because you could fall over them. (Cat 5)
First boy	It's fun though. It occupies your time and saves you fighting and nicking people's things. (Cat 6)
First girl	People could take your cars. (Cat 7)
First boy	Who's interested in cars? (aggressively) (Cat 20)
Second boy	Nobody have ever nicked your marbles. (Cat 20)
First boy	They do, cus I brought some and someone nicked um. (Cat 22)

Here the discussion is only partially concentrated on the task. The children move rapidly away from discussing the school rules towards inventing some of their own and there are more examples of non-cooperative behaviour where the boys, in particular, take the discussion away from the main point, their aggressive interventions preventing the other pupils in the group from bringing the task to a successful conclusion.

It should be emphasised that the schedule itself was not used live in the classroom. For scanning purposes a modified version of Figure 7.1 was used in which the pupils in the group were recorded in terms of the major categories at five-minute intervals over a twenty-minute period. For the most part teachers tended to rely on writing an impressionistic account of particular happenings during the group activity which might include small extracts of conversations or particularly interesting answers to questions. The categories in Figure 7.1 were then embedded into these descriptions. This approach is somewhat similar to that described by Michael Armstrong (1980) who

> tried to record in some detail what seemed to me on reflection to be the most significant events of the day, together with my observations, interpretations and speculations about them. Sometimes I wrote down everything I could recall that day, more often I chose to discuss particular incidents, children or pieces of work, whatever seemed to bear most directly on the character of the children's learning.
>
> (Armstrong 1980: 8)

In this way, therefore, teachers, like Armstrong were trying to convey not only the 'bald facts' of the situation but also the feeling of what it was like to participate in it. Anecdotes and near verbatim accounts of exchanges with pupils therefore became important. Unlike Armstrong, however, such accounts were also expressed within a shared set of understandings about the different processes and roles which pupils were expected to undertake when collaborating in group activity.

Thus in contrast to the earlier impressionistic account (pp. 155–6) one teacher wrote of some children in a discussion on the topic of school rules.

> Alexander's behaviour was mostly as an active participant, occasionally as a leader and on one occasion disruptive. He seems keen to tell of his past and unfortunate present circumstances whenever he can. Shows leadership by summarising and reading through the directions to make sure they were making progress and obeying instructions. Amanda also participated actively with some leadership behaviour. This was mainly shown in the way that she controls Alex's tendency to digress on school uniform, at one point. Nicola behaves very similarly to Amanda without exhibiting much evidence of leadership but whenever

possible attempts to move the discussion on by co-ordinating and summarising.

Vimi Rouak and Mitch say little or nothing and contribute no serious points to the discussion apart from when I am present with the group and ask them to speak. They are supportive rather than saboteurs although when questioned at the reporting back stage there is evidence that they have listened closely to the discussion and that they felt involved.

The categories also had another important use as they helped to develop among the teachers a collective notion of how a pupil's performance might be evaluated as someone who possessed the necessary skills to work effectively within a group. Effective group work required pupils to be able to display, at one time or another, in appropriate settings, leadership, negotiation and supportive roles. The instrument could then be used as a diagnostic measure so that in discussion with the pupils, not only could they gain a clear idea of what was expected of them on future occasions but also they clarified with the teacher his or her expectations of what was understood by 'working in groups'.

Thus, in one instance where a teacher had selected a small extract of the tape on school rules for analysis, the profile shown in Table 7.1 emerged under the main category headings.

Although it might be argued that the teacher might, from an impressionistic account of this behaviour, conclude that the main active participants were the girls rather than the boys, the more detailed analysis enabled the data in Table 7.1 to be used for

Table 7.1 Profile of pupil participation in a discussion on school rules

	Leadership	*Active participant*	Willing followers	Non-cooperation
Sarah	2, 4, 3, 4, 2	5	11	—
Bridget	3, 4	10, 3, 9	11, 13	—
Lee-anne	1, 2	5, 6	11	—
Colin		5, 8	11, 16	—
Matthew		5, 6, 8	11	—
Brendon			11, 12, 16	—

diagnostic purposes so that the boys were encouraged to participate more and the girls, particularly Sarah, requested to take less active roles on future occasions to give others a chance to practise group work skills.

In summary, therefore, teachers throughout the course of the study developed procedures for monitoring the working of groups in the classroom. Systematic observation was used to monitor the extent to which individual pupils in different contexts engaged in authority, negotiating and supportive roles within the group as well as identifying instances of non-functional behaviour. More detailed use of the categories within these major headings served two purposes. The first use was as a series of descriptors when teachers were writing impressionistic accounts of group activities. The second use was on occasions when teachers were uncertain about what was taking place in the group, as for example where there were no clear tangible outcomes but children were required to discuss ideas. Then a taped recording would be made, coupled on occasions with photographs of the proceedings. The unedited recording would be used to gain an overall impression and selections would then be transcribed for more detailed analysis using the category system. In this way the data collected could be used to provide what was earlier termed *critical feedback* about the performance of the whole group and of its individual members during a particular activity. The process served also to clarify for pupils the expectations which the teachers had concerning such group activity.

PUPILS' ROLE IN THE MONITORING PROCESS

The processes described in the previous section were all developed prior to the introduction of the National Curriculum with the added pressures on teachers to carry out regular assessments across a range of attainment targets in core subject areas. Advice on how to deliver this curriculum, such as that given by the writers of the non-statutory guidance on implementing the primary curriculum, tends to stress the importance of helping children to work effectively in groups but has little to say on how to implement such proposals successfully or how teachers might deal with the organisational problems of building up a group's sense of social identity.

Many of the teachers in ORACLE II, largely because they

believed in a 'skills embedded' rather than a 'skill training' approach tended to give little importance to the pupil's role in monitoring their own group performance. Evidence from studies both in the United States and in Australia suggests that such an evaluation by the pupils is an important part of building up the group's social identity. As Aronson *et al.* (1978) argue, while pupils usually have the idea that it is unacceptable to shout or punch each other, they have little understanding of the positive actions required to promote a good group atmosphere. Aronson and colleagues suggest a brain-storming session on the question 'How should we behave to help the group work more effectively?' Following this brain-storming the suggestions are posted up in the classroom in order of priority according to the rankings made by different groups. Whenever possible the behaviours are stated positively rather than negatively, since Aronson argues

> A student learns more by thinking about what he ought to be doing such as listening while another member is talking than he does by thinking about what he ought not to be doing such as not talking while someone else is speaking.
>
> (Aronson *et al.* 1978: 41)

In the above example students might then go on to list ways in which they should show each other they are listening. With the help of the teacher the pupils could compile a list which might look like the following.

1 Look directly at the speaker.
2 Nod that you understand him/her.
3 Rephrase what the speaker has just said.
4 Summarise the speaker's statements.
5 Reflect the feeling behind the statements (for example, when James says, 'I don't think we will ever finish at this rate', Diane might reflect 'It sounds like you're discouraged by our getting off the subject'.
6 Let the speaker know that you have heard by building on the ideas (e.g. I think what you have said is . . .).
7 Lean towards the speaker while listening.
8 Smile sometimes to reassure the speaker that what he/she is saying makes sense to you.

According to Aronson this approach helps pupils realise

that they themselves are able to develop a co-operative learning environment. They now have specific standards by which to recognise, diagnose and cope with problems constructively so that they will be able to try effectively to be able to change the group process to make it more rewarding.

(Aronson et al. 1978: 42)

For such evaluations it is important that pupils write their impressions of the group rather than just think about them. Aronson argues that writing down an evaluation increases pupils' motivation to examine the group process and to commit themselves to improving it. He and his colleagues recommend that each pupil write his or her individual opinion first and then join the others in filling out a group card. In this way each pupil will have something specific to share with others since 'without the chance to write their opinions first pupils often merely say that everything is "O.K." or "not bad" and let it go at that' (Aronson et al. 1978: 42). The advantage of filling in cards in this way is that it not only allows the pupils a chance to see where they might improve their collaborative activity but also prevents them from not focusing on ways in which they are already working well, thus denying them the opportunity for positive reinforcement.

In the Australian example (Reid et al. 1982), a more general evaluative checklist, shown in Figure 7.2, is used. Again it is recommended that the individual pupils in the group fill out a separate sheet first before coming together and arriving at an overall evaluation. Reid and her colleagues do, in extreme circumstances, where there is dominance or disruption, recommend direct teacher intervention. For example, where a pupil is seen by others to be too dominant they may be asked to be a Chairperson in the next discussion or a timekeeper for an experiment. In the initial stages of group work she accepts that disruptive pupils may have to be isolated while recognising that in this situation the pupil has less opportunity to experience co-operative behaviour and to come to appreciate the value of working in a group. Once the majority of the class is working well in a collaborative situation it may be possible for the teacher to place several of the more disruptive students together and then spend more time with that group. In general, like the American researchers, Reid and her colleagues argue that a need for such extreme intervention by the teacher will be rare providing the

WHAT HAPPENED?

Communication   YES   NO
1 Did all group members feel free to talk?
2 Was there any interrupting or cutting off?
3 Did people listen to one another?
4 Were group members asked to expand a point
   they were trying to make?

Participation
5 Did all members have opportunities to share
   their ideas?
6 Did any member(s) dominate?
7 Were group members sensitive to the needs and
   concerns of other group members?

Decision-making
8 Did the group consider a number of ideas before
   coming to a decision?
9 Did everyone agree to the decisions that were
   made?
10 Was there any organisation in the group?

Figure 7.2 Pupil behaviour during group activity

general principles which have been established in earlier parts of
this book are followed. They recommend, for example, that
teachers 'should tell students what they are going to be doing and
why – sharing with them the learning theory of working in
groups' (Reid *et al.* 1982: 35). They also recommend that all tasks
should initially be short and very specific such as 'making a
group list or leaving out the last paragraph of the story and
asking the pupils to predict the ending' (Reid *et al.* 1982: 38) and,
like Aronson *et al.* (1978), they suggest that initially pupils should
be encouraged to 'brain-storm' in formulating their own rules for
group discussion. A further exercise in self-evaluation, once the
group has begun to work collaboratively, is for their teacher to
produce a list of characteristics of effective and ineffective groups
which students can use to compare with their own evaluations.
Interestingly, Reid *et al.*'s (1982) list of effective characteristics of
groups tends to focus much more on how pupils feel rather than
what they do so that, for example, positive features include the
following:

There is disagreement in the group and the group is comfortable with this. They work together towards sorting it out and nobody *feels* unhappy with the decisions made.

People *feel* free to criticise and say honestly what they think. Everybody knows how everybody else *feels* about what is being discussed.

This again supports the arguments developed earlier and is consistent with the intuitive approach adopted by Jean Wright as described in Chapter 5. These and other studies not only claim that the role of pupils in monitoring their own performance enhances the student's understanding of how groups work but also stress the responsibility of pupils for controlling their own learning. When pupils are asked to focus their attention on the process of learning within the small group they gain better understandings and hence a greater control of both the learning taking place and of the ways in which they can make their group work more effectively.

8

CHANGING CLASSROOM PRACTICE

TEACHERS AND CLASSROOM RESEARCH

This chapter examines the effectiveness of some of the strategies which are likely to be used when a school or, in a wider context, a local authority, attempts to persuade classroom teachers to make fundamental changes in their classroom practice. Such a change might involve, for example, a decision to adopt the kinds of teaching strategies advocated in the previous chapters to increase the proportion of collaborative group work taking place. If the research evidence is to be believed, such decisions taken in the primary school rarely lead to successful innovation. The ORACLE research of the mid-1970s (Galton *et al.* 1980) described classrooms which were, typically, the same as those investigated by Mortimore *et al.* (1988) and Tizard *et al.* (1988). In between this period other studies, admittedly in small, mainly rural schools (Galton and Patrick 1990), also demonstrated that similar patterns of classroom organisation and of pupil–teacher interaction extended across all types of schools at both infant and junior level. Primary classroom practice seems, therefore, to have remained remarkably stable during the 1980s.

This same period, however, has been marked by a number of attempts to change existing classroom practice in the primary school using what have come to be known as the 'action research' approach. In the most recent of these, Alexander *et al.* (1989) the researchers were unable to find evidence of any substantial shift in teaching style in spite of expenditure by the local authority to support the innovation of the order of several million pounds. An 'action research' approach was also adopted in the Leverhulme-sponsored STAR project, a jointly funded programme which took place at the Universities of Liverpool and Leicester. This also failed to demonstrate, by means of before and after observation, that any substantial shift of teaching style had taken place although the evidence suggested that, by the end of the project, teachers had gained a much deeper understanding of the nature of primary science activity and were better able to evaluate pupil performance across a range of classroom process skills (Cavendish *et al.* 1990). The ORACLE II programme, *Effective Group Work in the Primary Classroom*, also adopted an 'action research' approach and yet we have seen, particularly in local authority B, where the main study took place, that there was little increase in the proportion of collaborative activity within the classes of the experimental group.

To some, however, 'action research' seems to be the only way of improving classroom practice. Thus Hustler *et al.* (1986) in a book on the topic begin by stating

> There is no doubt that nearly everyone with a direct interest in classroom teaching is disenchanted with traditional educational research. Whether they be teachers or teacher educators, HMI's or LEA Advisers, Heads of schools or Heads of Departments, they regard such research as lacking in relevance and practicability for what they all regard as the prime task: helping teachers to improve the learning experience of children in their classes. This is not to say that these parties see no need for research. They do, and plenty of it, for the problems are many and pressing. But it must be research which is positive, leading to action in the classroom and can help with these problems.
>
> (Hustler *et al.* 1986: 7)

In developing their arguments, Hustler and his colleagues point to the pioneering research of the Ford Teaching Project based at the Centre for Applied Research in Education (CARE) in the University of East Anglia as a source of 'some very influential collaborative research strategies'. However, it is the work of Elliott (1980) and the Schools Council's Teacher–Pupil Interaction and the Quality of Learning (TIQL) project which it is claimed enabled 'action research to spread out beyond those who had direct contact either with CARE or the Cambridge Institute' (Hustler *et al.* 1986: 4). Hustler *et al.* also cite as an important influence the work of Kemmis and colleagues at Deakin University,

Australia, particularly two publications by Grundy and Kemmis (1981) and by Carr and Kemmis (1986).

It is not the intention here to deny the value of the 'teacher as researcher' movement as originally developed by the late Lawrence Stenhouse, from which the action research approach, as used in Australia and the United Kingdom, developed. But we are concerned about the kind of exaggerated claims made for this particular form of action research and particularly the kind of polarisation which the most ardent advocates wish to establish between what they call 'traditional research' and their particular form of classroom-based inquiry. Indeed, Hustler *et al.*'s (1986) claim that everyone, including LEAs, are disenchanted with traditional research is not borne out by one of the leading practitioners of action research, in his account of the projects which is claimed to be a key element in the development of action research practice. Writing about the problems and dilemmas which emerged during the Teacher–Pupil Interaction and the Quality of Learning Project (TIQL) the director, John Elliott, reveals there was considerable concern expressed by one LEA adviser that 'the research element seems to me to be pretty nebulous'. At the same time other members of the Steering Committee argued that allowing the teachers to define the focus of the research, a key element in the action research ideology, 'was likely to result in a diversity of concerns and a resulting incoherence in outcomes' (Elliott 1985: 249).

It may be that the kinds of strategies developed during the ORACLE II, Effective Group Work in the Primary Classroom, project and the Leverhulme, Science Teaching Action Research (STAR) project, did not conform to the rather narrow definitions of action research proposed by Elliott (1985) and Carr and Kemmis (1986). However, it is interesting that the reservations expressed by the LEA advisers and the TIQL project sponsors concerning the lack of focus and coherence, the failure to crystallise aims, the slowness of the teachers to develop any programme of action which would allow any identified outcome to emerge were all identified by Williamson and a team of seconded teachers during the year in which they acted as external evaluators to the ORACLE II project. Elliott, however, rejects what he sees as pressures 'to control teachers' thinking by providing a more structured approach to such projects', arguing that it would

CHANGING CLASSROOM PRACTICE

'thereby distort rather than enable the processes of first-order action research to take place' (Elliott 1986: 259).

In a later paper, Elliott (1989), like Hustler and his colleagues, strongly rejects the value of ideas about teaching developed through traditional empirical, psychological research such as that carried out in the ORACLE studies. He cites with approval an article by Kroath (1989) who attempted to persuade teachers to replace 'the deficient elements in their subjective theory' with formal psychological theory as a basis for changing practice. Kroath reported that the experiment made no impact on the teachers' 'subjective' theory and that the teachers reported that they did not intend to change any aspect of their practice although they found the exercise a 'stimulating experience'. In commenting on Kroath's account Elliott (1989: 95) concludes that the approach failed because it encouraged the teachers to see teaching as a 'technical rational activity of applying instrumental rules derived from theory rather than as a moral activity of real-ising values in the activity as a whole'. Kroath's (1989) conclusion is that research on teaching based on empirical studies of the classroom process has little to contribute to the development of teachers' thinking about their own practice, unless such teachers have arrived at a point in their own development where they themselves see the need for this theoretical input. This is a de-pressing conclusion because it appears to offer no solution to the problems raised in the previous paragraphs concerning the time scale of change and the resolution of views held by different groups of teachers with different ideological perspectives which give rise to discontinuity and lack of focus during action research.

It perhaps needs to be pointed out that there is no general agreement on the definition of what constitutes action research, although all agree that it seeks to translate emerging theory into demonstratable effective practice. According to Covey (1953) the term was first used by Kurt Lewin to describe the process of planning, executing and reflecting in order to gain 'deeper in-sights into the laws that govern social life'. This process of self-reflection is, according to Cohen and Manion (1980), character-ised by four features. First, the research is situational, in that it is concerned with diagnosing a problem in a specific context. Second, it tends to be collaborative with teams of researchers and practitioners working together. Third, it is participatory so that

173

the team members themselves take part directly in implementing the research, and fourth, it is self-evaluative in that modifications are continually evaluated within the ongoing situation with the ultimate intention to improve practice. There is nothing in this more generalised definition of action research which precludes the use of theories about teaching, derived from empirical study, as a basis for changing classroom practice and Kroath's (1989) account of his attempt to use such theory seems remarkably insensitive, given that the teachers had spent considerable time developing a number of hypotheses prior to being informed that these disagreed with existing psychological evidence. In what follows, therefore, we will examine the way in which empirical theory can be used to inform classroom practice without alienating the teachers and also look at other possible ways of integrating an 'action research' approach with other forms of in-service provision. First, however, we shall describe the ORACLE II experience.

THE ORACLE II EXPERIENCE

As described in Chapter 2, the main thrust of the ORACLE II programme in local authority B where the main experiment took place consisted of a two-stage 'action research' style programme. In the first stage, a group of teachers who were all interested in improving the quality of collaborative group work in their classrooms came together to see how this might best be done. During this stage the project team acted as the consultants. In Stage 2, this group of teachers now worked with another group to see whether the ideas, developed in Stage 1, could be implemented successfully by other colleagues who were, perhaps working under different conditions and in different contexts. In this second stage the first group of teachers now, therefore, acted as the consultants. When presented to the second group of teachers, the ideas of the first group were offered as a set of hypothesises about how groups of children could collaborate effectively in the primary classroom and were not to be seen as a set of prescriptions. Although, therefore, there were differences in approaches between the two stages, all teachers involved in this programme shared a common commitment to examine their own classroom practice by

174

1 developing appropriate methods of classroom observation
2 using these methods systematically to record the information about their classroom practice
3 evaluating the aims of this practice in the light of these observations.

In our analysis of the 'action research' approach, however, we shall concentrate mainly on the first stage of the project. This is because at Stage 2 the programme had to be altered somewhat for reasons explained in Chapter 2. At Stage 1, however, the group of twenty teachers involved was able to spend the better part of a year attempting to develop collaborative group work in their own classrooms by identifying key issues connected with group work, such as the size of groups, the nature of tasks, etc. and evaluating the effect of variation in these measures upon the degree of collaboration among pupils. The project team supported the work of the teachers in a number of ways. They acted as a second pair of hands, freeing the teacher to spend time in concentrating on a particular group of pupils. They acted as observers on occasions either carrying out systematic observation or filming and recording particular events. The project provided additional resources, particularly secretarial support, for transcribing audio tapes and also organised in-service meetings which were held monthly throughout the year with the support of the local authority.

At the same time the group of four headteachers, who were on a one-year secondment studying management, were prevailed upon to act as evaluators under the direction of one of the authors, John Williamson, who was on a year's sabbatical leave. The following extracts from one of the teacher evaluator's notes gives some indication of the difficulties and frustrations experienced by the Stage 1 teachers as they attempted to research their own classrooms.

The group was assembled by 9.30 a.m. The room was buzzing with conversation. We looked at some video extracts of collaborative group work which had been recorded previously. In the discussion which followed some of the issues highlighted concerned problems of dealing with large numbers of groups, particularly children who came to watch or came for help or what to do about groups who were obviously not working but didn't come to help.

Pressures on the teacher appeared to affect the quality of his interaction with the group (e.g. the teacher was distracted and turned his head away from a pupil just as he had questioned her without waiting for an answer). After lunch the teachers went into their jig-saw groups to prepare a chart which highlighted the issues which would be explored during the following month. Again I was impressed by the cohesive nature of the group as exemplifed by the contributions everyone made, the way they listened to each other and the way they discussed issues and arrived at a consensus after an examination of each other's views. The main issue highlighted for further study was the use of time since this was seen to be crucial to the amount of pupil teacher interaction and the organisation of the physical environment. It was decided to collect evidence of the allocation of time in the classroom by use of tick sheets to monitor the demands made by the child and by the teacher.

(7 October)

When the Stage 1 teachers next met, the evaluator, however, reported that

First of all they discussed the work they had carried out in trying to pin point the areas in which the children had made the most demands on teachers' time. There had been a number of practical difficulties in using their tick sheets. The teachers either had to stay at their desks or carry the sheets round and some of the categories were too wide which made the analysis difficult. On a more practical level, some schools had had staffing problems which meant that for part of the time classes had doubled up and there had been coming and going of children from withdrawal groups. Most teachers concluded that a day's observation was too short and they suggested that next time they would record over a week to show the variation in the day's activities and the resulting demands from children. Attention was then focused on the question of feedback centring on three issues, how to obtain it, how much of it and what quality. The group gradually worked on a framework which would allow them to categorise both verbal and non-verbal forms of feedback when watching video recordings. Towards the end of the day, one of the research team

176

reported on the work of all of the different groups. This was valuable ensuring that the work embarked upon over the next month would not be a repeat of that already undertaken and also ensured that each group would fit in with the ideas of the other group with not too many overlaps.

(28 October)

A month later the evaluator recorded that

The group met the previous week to look over video recordings in order to choose something suitable for their INSET day. They had devoted two hours to the task eventually finding a tape they considered good for their purpose.

The tape was then shown to all the teachers but this second viewing produced a completely different effect on the group who had selected it. It was now seen that there was too little teacher-pupil interaction to make sensible judgements and that the camera always seemed to focus on something else when it was necessary to decide on the context. Previously the group had admired the calm approach used by the teacher but on this second viewing they considered he was too 'neutral' and that interactions took place with too few children. After a little time the video was abandoned and the group began to discuss the reasons for their dissatisfaction with the film, the inappropriateness of the monitoring sheet for feedback and the effect the course was having on the way they saw things now. The difficulty of monitoring the classroom was still seen as a major problem. The group explored the possibility of children being able to record contact time with the teacher. There was little evidence that feedback was of a thought-provoking kind. It mostly consisted of brief comments on work or instructions. The group therefore decided to clarify further their ideas on what constituted 'good feedback'. Everyone considered that time had been well spent in understanding both the causes and the problem itself and recognising the implications for both teachers and pupils. What was needed now, the group concluded, was to consider what to do about the problem.

(25 November)

This was the last meeting before Christmas. At this stage there was little attempt to formulate ideas about what constituted

177

effective group work. Instead teachers concentrated on the more practical problem of collecting and recording data about their classrooms which might form the basis for such theorising. At the first meeting of the spring term

> The group divided into smaller groups to discuss the happenings of the previous month: particularly the attempts to focus on the quality of feedback given to children and the effect this had on pupil behaviour in the groups. Some teachers had been focusing, in particular, on the amount and quality of feedback given to children during mathematics. Everyone agreed that interaction with children was still chiefly when the pupils had got something wrong. They further agreed that they must persist with their work despite the present limitations. Future plans were concerned with ways of getting children to monitor the group interaction which the teacher was prevented from seeing because he or she was occupied elsewhere but it was decided that the children's monitoring would be carried out over two weeks but only the second week's results would be analysed because it was felt that by then the novelty would have worn off and the children would not be just looking for happenings to be recorded. After lunch Maurice took stock of the situation as he saw it and dealt with the group's anxiety about getting results. He re-emphasised the long term nature of the problem but reiterated the gains in confidence and the openness in talking to each other which now characterised all the groups. He echoed their hopes that this would be replicated in the staff rooms in all the schools and also thought that during the meetings we had increased our ability to see issues more clearly.

> (12 January)

In these four extracts we see the development of at least two cycles of action research. In the first the Stage 1 teachers were concerned in how better to organise time in order to afford themselves the freedom to monitor group activity. In their attempts to 'research' this issue they are beset by numerous problems, for example, the difficulty of recording suitable video material to illustrate what they believed to be effective practice. It appears that what was perceived as good practice turns out, on closer examination, to be less effective than first thought. Examination

178

of the available video tapes, however, begins to change the focus of the teachers' inquiry into the effect of giving feedback. Although methods for recording feedback are offered by the team, the teachers prefer to develop their own classification and to examine how different forms of feedback appear to affect the way that pupils respond within the group. They note, in particular, as the cartoon pictures previously identified, that much of the feedback offered consisted of critical comments whenever pupils gave incorrect answers.

It could be argued, from this account, that there is evidence of teachers' theorising about group work. Although they never solve the recording problem they were moving to a position which accorded with the research findings concerning the effects of evaluative and critical feedback presented in Chapter 6. However, by the next meeting in February Stage 1 teachers were under considerable pressure to produce more concrete results. This pressure came not from the project team, who in the previous evaluation meeting had reassured them of the value of what had been accomplished, but by their headteachers. On the day prior to the February meeting the Project Director met the headteachers to discuss progress. General dissatisfaction was expressed at the lack of any concrete results which could be fed back to the other teachers in the school. As one headteacher remarked,

> I have governors and parents on my back. Yvonne is seen by them to be one of the better teachers and they are unhappy that the children in her class are deprived of her presence one day a month. I find it difficult to justify her absence when they ask me what the school is gaining. Telling them that she's trying to find out how to make children work better in groups doesn't help. They reply, 'What has she found then?' and I am at a loss to answer.

Yet there existed, even at that time, a considerable wealth of what the critics called 'traditional' psychological research evidence which might have helped to speed up the action research process and also provided the headteacher with an answer for the parents and governors. It is not certain that all ORACLE II teachers shared the views expressed by those in Kroath's (1989) account. In his report of the TIQL project, for example, Elliott (1985) also states that one school withdrew because it felt that the aims of the study were not sufficiently clear. In Australia action research programmes have reported that teachers expressed similar feelings of frustration because of the slow rate of progress.

Those responsible for such programmes appear to assume that if teachers change their views of themselves when participating in action research this will automatically lead to changes in their classroom practice. This transformation is seen as a three-stage process. First teachers undergo a process of reorientation which leads them to look at their role in a different way. This leads to the second stage where teachers attempt to change the classroom climate which in turn makes it possible for teachers to begin the third stage and change their practice to fit the new classroom ethos. However, from their writings, it is clear that the action research facilitators often have in their minds a very clear understanding about the 'correct climate' which is required to bring about the desired changes in teaching style. Experience suggests that during the project teachers are then likely to be subjected to a form of 'guided discovery' in which they have to work out for themselves what it is the consultants already thought and wanted them to do. According to Williamson (1988) teachers often complain about this process, stating that since the consultants had expert knowledge which enabled them to formulate appropriate teaching strategies, it would have been more helpful and saved everyone considerable time and effort if this knowledge had been disclosed earlier. It is not therefore axiomatic, as the action research paradigm appears to suggest, that teachers need to discover the theory for themselves.

In an extended literature review Williamson (1988) failed to find any detailed accounts of longitudinal action research projects where theorising of the kind approved by Kroath (1989) had taken place. Most of the studies cited rarely got beyond the first cycle of actual data collection and tentative hypothesising. In this form, therefore, action research appears to help teachers develop a better understanding of the actual learning process taking place, what might be termed a theory of *classroom activity*. However, none of the studies demonstrated that teachers moved beyond their existing practice to develop explanations of how the learning process might be changed by the use of different teaching styles thereby formulating a theory of *classroom practice*.

In the ORACLE II project traditional theory was finally introduced and accepted by some teachers in local authority C once the consultant had engaged in the action alongside the teacher. This leads to an alternative hypothesis that the teachers reject psychological theory not, as Elliott (1989) argues because they regarded it as technocratic, but because they do not have confidence that the consultant sees the problem from the perspective of someone who is inside the action. Consequently, they doubt whether such theory would be relevant to their immediate practical concerns.

THE TEACHER AS RESEARCHER

As it has developed in the United Kingdom version of action research, the relationship between the teacher-researcher and the consultant-researcher has been presented as one in which the two partners in the research each complement each other's expertise. The teacher-researcher possesses practical knowledge of the classroom which the consultant lacks. Having decided on an approach the teacher then seeks, with the help of the consultant, to explain why such methods are effective. The consultant's role is to supply the expertise necessary to help this process whereby the teacher moves from observation to reflection. The unwritten rule appears to be that the consultant offers this expertise only when asked to do so by the teacher. Thus, for example, in the illustrative film made by the Ford Teaching Project team, *Fish in a Tank*, the teacher and the consultant sit down to watch a recorded tape/slide sequence of a lesson. The decision whether to stop the tape and discuss a particular episode is left entirely to the teacher. Only if the teacher asks for it is the consultant's opinion given. In *Fish in a Tank*, for example, the teacher decides that the failure of the pupils to develop their investigation independently is a result of excessive teacher guidance resulting in too rapid a switch from the children's interest to that of the teacher. The consultant, who has also interviewed the children and confirmed this viewpoint, reveals this fact only after agreeing with the teacher's analysis. Presumably if the teacher had not stopped the tape no such analysis would have taken place.

One reason for this limitation of the consultant's participation is that it minimises the risk to the teacher's self-esteem by, in effect, establishing a clear demarcation between each participant's role, based upon the different skills possessed by the teacher and the consultant. Such an analysis may, however, be

181

problematic. Among any group of teachers it is often possible to gain some impression of the likely effectiveness of colleagues, even though they are meeting outside a classroom. Similarly teachers, who might have met the consultant in another capacity (as tutor of an in-service programme, for example), may form an opinion about the consultant's teaching expertise because it is thought that generic skills of teaching extend beyond a particular context. When this happens and a favourable judgement is made, then the intervention of the consultant is likely to be more acceptable than in the case where a teacher does not rate highly the consultant's pedagogic skills. This was illustrated, quite dramatically, during ORACLE II, when one of the researchers, who had never trained as a teacher, offered to take over the class only to finish the day with the best paint brushes stuck in the glue pot. Thereafter, the contribution of this person's undoubted research expertise to the pedagogic debate was always marginal. When, however, a consultant is perceived to possess effective teaching skills teachers may find it difficult to understand why he or she stands back from giving necessary help in theorising about observed practice. This may account, in part, for the frustration felt by some participating teachers in action research programmes at the lack of clear aims and guidance.

One solution to these difficulties is, as happened in local authority C, for the consultant and teacher to exchange roles. Some of the most significant advances relating to the analysis of the tasks in terms of Doyle's (1983) theory of risk and ambiguity and of Deci and Ryan's (1985) linkage between the management of learning and the management of behaviour came only when the consultant abandoned the role of facilitator and reactant and became instead a teacher-researcher in the school. Part of the reason for this progress was the change in the relationship as the consultant became a continual physical presence in the school rather than someone who came occasionally in order to observe or to discuss the teachers' reflections. This change in relationship was illustrated on one occasion when a teacher, studying for an advanced degree, sought the consultant's help over a dissertation. On this occasion before their meeting the teacher concerned, who was partial to garlic sausage, went round colleagues seeking a strong mint to neutralise her breath. Similar precautions were not taken the next day, however, when the discussion concerned the group work project. Sharing teaching seemed, therefore, to be a 'humanising' and 'equalising' experience for *all* participants in the action research. The teachers at Burwood gained confidence from the fact that the consultant, although not so inadequate as to require them to hide the paintbrushes, nevertheless needed and was grateful for their support on occasions. This in turn appeared to make it easier for them to accept the advice and help of the consultant when they attempted to identify problems and to theorise about practice.

Another important aspect of this changed role for the consultant was that it enabled the teachers' and pupils' behaviour to be studied on a day-to-day basis. In particular, as the relationship with the pupils developed, it became possible to gain insights into the way in which they viewed the school and their teachers, insights which could not have been obtained from questionnaires or interviews. At the same time, the consultant's knowledge of the relevant research was important since it directed attention to likely areas where, for example, fear of failure would be prevalent, such as reading aloud or discussing in groups.

Again, the training received in earlier ORACLE studies as a participant observer helped the consultant in switching roles. Elsewhere Delamont (1983) has commented on the fact that during the transfer study she, as a trained observer, filled a notebook when observing one lesson, whereas some of the teachers involved could manage only half a page. Part of the Stage 1 teachers' problem, as it appeared in the extracts from the headteacher's evaluation report of ORACLE II, was their inability to focus on key questions. The same difficulties were expressed by the teachers in the TIQL project (Elliott 1985). Eventually, in ORACLE II, the attempts by the consultant to negotiate with pupils which, as recounted in Galton (1989), at first proved a disaster, made possible much deeper discussions with the teachers who, although willing to try similar negotiations, preferred, initially, to learn from the consultant's experience. Even so, such fundamental changes were only just beginning at the end of five years. No doubt they would have continued but at the end of that year the headteacher departed to take up a new post as an adviser and three of the teachers left, including Jean Wright, two to take up posts as deputy headteachers in other schools and the third to become an advisory teacher. Within one term, under the direction of a new headteacher, the experiments in negotiation had ceased and teacher-directed control was again in evidence. It could be argued that the teachers who left carried with them their new ideas and practices and were able to take several short cuts in arriving at a similar position with their new colleagues. The experience of ORACLE II and similar projects, however, suggests that the action research approach needs substantial modification if these time-scales are to be reduced.

The shift in the methodology governing action research, particularly the changed role of the consultant from facilitator to collaborator, has also been endorsed by Kemmis (1989). Originally, he and his colleagues saw themselves as 'facilitators' and 'moderators' who offered 'advice and support on research techniques' but were

> also beginning to offer theoretical perspectives which could link the work the researchers were doing to relevant literature about their substantive problems and about ideology. We still believed that we should not intervene too strongly lest the researchers lose intellectual control of their own research work.

> (Kemmis 1989: 22)

However, Kemmis and colleagues, having reviewed their theory and their practice of action research, have now come to see this 'them and us' relationship as a self-deception. They concluded from their analysis that their 'non-intervention frequently deprived the teacher-researchers of relevant sources of theory' and that by structuring the work in this way 'it became excessively pragmatic' (Kemmis 1989: 21). Moreover, when as 'facilitators and moderators' they did offer technical or theoretical support, a contradiction in their role became apparent. When offering these suggestions Kemmis and his team then confronted college staff with their own differences and competing and conflicting interests so that as consultants they were 'perceived as spokespersons for a particular approach, not as acting neutrally towards any and all suggestions' (Kemmis 1989: 24). Kemmis's conclusion is that approaches to action research, which rely heavily on an 'individualistic theory of empowerment' confront consultants with a 'difficult and somewhat hypocritical position', one where 'they wish to share the commitment but refuse to accept the final responsibility for action' (Kemmis 1989: 22) and this is a view we would endorse. In a number of case studies Kemmis (1989) illustrates this shift towards more collaborative activity which, although it does not include our suggestion that teachers and consultants should exchange roles in the classroom, offers a number of useful ways in which the 'them and us' relationship, originally postulated as a central feature of the 'teacher as research' paradigm, can be broken down.

ALTERNATIVE APPROACHES TO CLASSROOM CHANGE

In the United States there are those, such as Joyce and Showers (1980), who have argued that a more direct coaching approach can bring about quicker change in classroom practice. They claim that such coaching should include the presentation of relevant theory, a demonstration of how such theory translates to classroom practice, a period of actual practice followed by feedback under 'safe' conditions followed by classroom application. This strategy is described as a 'coaching' approach because it is similar to the method that coaches use to hone the skills of athletes. It is based upon the principle that if a complex task is reduced to a series of simple steps and a training programme devised that guarantees success at each step then teachers will be more likely to persevere in their attempts to incorporate such practice into their normal classroom routines. For example, in seeking to improve class teaching by means of the coaching approach the use of advanced organisers (Ausubel 1978) to structure an introduction to a lesson would be demonstrated by the trainer or presented in the form of a teaching vignette. The teacher would then be given a different topic and asked to present it to the remainder of the group using an advanced organiser. This presentation could be video taped and the trainer would then provide the teacher with feedback on his or her performance. The process could be repeated until the desired level of competence was achieved. The teacher would then try out the process under normal classroom conditions. Having mastered the use of the advanced organiser the teacher would then move to the next stage of the 'direct instruction' model involving 'concept acquisition'.

Thus the approach has five main components.

1 Presenting a theory or a description of skills or a strategy.
2 Modelling or demonstrating these skills or the teaching derived from the theory.

3 Practising these new teaching approaches in simulated class-room settings.
4 Providing structured and open-ended feedback on the performance in the simulated setting.
5 Coaching for application involving classroom assistance with the transfer of the new skills and strategies to the normal classroom.

This coaching model is claimed to enjoy considerable success in the United States (Joyce and Showers 1983).

Critics of this coaching approach, however, argue that it works less well when the tasks involved are complex and cannot be broken down into discrete steps. Unlike 'action research', where the teacher learns a general method which can be applied to all pedagogic problems, in the coaching model the method has to be specific. Learning, for example, how to present an advanced organiser does not help the teacher develop an effective way of teaching pupils to acquire a new concept. Williamson (1988) has, therefore, attempted to develop an approach which combines aspects of the action research model with that of the coaching approach. The programme was based on a series of weekly workshops where teachers not only acquired and practised new teaching strategies based upon relevant theory but also learnt how to operate elements of the action research cycle. Once they had mastered the new teaching strategies in the workshop they could plan, act, observe and reflect upon their application in the classroom context.

The strategies of teaching were first demonstrated to teachers and they were then coached to master them. Teachers were then asked to implement teaching strategies in the classroom and audio record the lesson. They were visited by a consultant who observed lessons and assisted in the implementation of the new teaching strategy. If necessary, the consultant provided further on-site coaching in order to raise the levels of performance.

Subsequent observation and lesson transcripts from a series of lessons demonstrated that teachers were able to master these new teaching strategies and to implement them in the classroom. For example, one teacher, using the enquiring training strategy developed by Joyce and Weil (1986), subsequently recorded a science lesson where the experiment consisted of pushing a can

186

down into water and observing the change in water level. Towards the end of the lesson the following exchange took place.

Teacher   Well, you saw what it read beforehand, didn't you? So, yes, it does make a difference when you put it in the water. You saw that. Peter?

Peter   When you put the can in the water, the pressure pushes it up and makes the level . . .

Teacher   What is this pressure that's pushing it up? You keep telling me it's pressure, but what pressure?

In the analysis of this lesson the teacher came to see that, in contrast to the method recommended in the enquiry training approach, she still retained close control throughout the discussion with the pupils. Two lessons later, however, after the teacher had listened to further transcripts of the lessons and discussed these with the consultant the element of control was considerably reduced.

Teacher   If you were in water, I don't know. So, Stuart and Leo, you reckon the most important thing on this whole experiment is what?

Leo   Gravity.

Teacher   Well done. How do you feel about this exercise?

Leo   I liked it because we did the experiment with different students on the ends of the rope.

Stuart   And with a shorter distance between the weight and the rope ends and heavier weights.

Teacher   Yes, but what was the most useful thing we did?

Leo   We were able to talk and then try the experiment to look at our ideas or theories.

Even though there has clearly been a shift in the teaching approach used subsequent discussion with the consultant indicates that the teacher will now engage in a further round of action research. She tells the consultant:

Firstly, at the beginning of the lesson, I ask students who had a hypothesis (I use the term theories with them) not to voice them until I asked for any. Upon reflection I feel that possibly this restricted somewhat the enquiry nature of the lesson in that students should be able to voice their opinions at any stage.

Secondly, at the conclusion of the lesson I referred to Leo's hypothesis by saying that it sounds like a pretty good theory and the class then took it to mean it was the correct one.

At this stage we should try to extend the hypothesis to other situations in order to formulate a 'true' theory.

It appears, therefore, that when an innovation was characterised by a concrete experience, coupled with active experimentation involving on-site coaching it was possible for teachers to acquire complex technical skills and incorporate these into an expanded repertoire of teaching strategies. All of the teachers involved in this project also reported a change in their beliefs and a deeper understanding about classroom processes and relationships. For the majority of teachers, therefore, the programme provided more than 'fine tuning' of previous knowledge or newly acquired skills. Rather it was perceived as a fundamental shift in their thinking about students' understanding of content and the way in which the teacher and students interacted in the classroom.

These ideas fit in well with more recent thinking about curriculum innovation in the primary school. For example, the recent Council of Europe project, *Curriculum Innovation in the Primary School* (CDCC 1987), devoted considerable attention to this issue. As reported in Galton and Blyth (1989), the project advocated a mixed approach in which outsiders when promoting innovation took account, at the earliest stage, of the constraints posed by the school context while, at the same time, teachers acknowledged that those sponsoring the innovation could contribute a wider perspective. An approach, very similar to that suggested by Williamson (1988), is described by Kopmels (1989) in his account of the Dutch experimental school which took part in the Council of Europe Project.

FACILITATING CHANGE IN THE CLASSROOM

Up to now the discussion might appear to suggest that the process of change is the same in all schools and for all teachers. Clearly this is not so. In the ORACLE II project and in Williamson's (1988) study the teachers were enthusiastic volunteers. Many of the studies of action research have taken place in schools belonging to the Classroom Action Research

Network (CARN) where it might be hypothesised that the teachers involved shared the philosophy and aims expressed by that organisation and were also enthusiastic change agents. What appears to be lacking is a step-by-step developmental model which can identify the degree to which a teacher is prepared to engage in the innovation. Given such knowledge it might then be possible to provide the most appropriate form of in-service experience to best facilitate change.

One attempt to construct such a developmental model has been made by Gene Hall and his associates and is described in some detail by Hord (1987). The model, the Concerns-Based Adoption Model (CBAM), identifies seven graded stages of concern through which an individual teacher passes during the process of implementing change. These stages are embedded within three levels. In the first level the main preoccupation is with *information* where individual teachers want to know more about the proposal. The second level deals with the more *personal* costs to the individual during which Doyle and Ponder's (1977) practicality ethic begins to operate. Teachers wish to know how the change will effect them personally and the management costs in terms of their time and their efforts. The third level involves what Hord (1987) calls *impact* concerns where teachers begin to examine ways in which the proposed change will affect others. Questions such as 'How are these changes affecting my pupils?' and 'How does what I am doing relate to what other teachers are doing?' become of paramount importance and lead to fresh ideas about developing alternative strategies that might work even better. Within the information, personal and impact levels there are, in all, seven stages of concern. For each of the seven specific stages of concern there are corresponding behaviours which allow each stage to be identified although Hord (1987) makes clear that there is not complete correspondence between the stages of concern and the levels of behaviour. For example, at the impact level the teacher might be making changes to increase either the quality or the quantity of pupils' outcomes or may be making deliberate efforts to co-operate with other teachers in using the innovation. Essentially, therefore, during change the teacher passes through a process of *initiation, consolidation* and *reorientation* and it is only at the latter stage when the teachers are strongly committed to the proposed change that the action research approach appears to work effectively.

THE MANAGEMENT OF CHANGE

The Council of Europe project, *Innovation in the Primary School* (CDCC 1987), gave considerable attention to the management of change within the school. Twelve schools, recommended by the participating countries as outstanding examples of innovation, were the subject of detailed case studies as part of what was called the Contact School Plan (Kopmels 1987). As part of the analysis, Kopmels developed what he called the five zones model of school improvement, the central feature of which concerned the fourth zone which dealt with the organisation of the co-operation of the teaching staff. This involved the style of leadership, the system of support and friendship between teachers within the school and the organisational structure which enabled all participants to feel some sense of ownership in the innovation.

As might be expected, the role of the school leader was seen to be a crucial one. Yet a wider survey of practice, within the primary schools within the Member States of the CDCC, provided a picture in which a constantly recurring theme was the breakdown of communication within the school itself as a major factor inhibiting innovation and change. Nearly 75 per cent of all the cases mentioned this effect, reporting that there were many problems in human relationships between staff within the institutions and between the school staff and the local authority advisers and inspectors. According to this survey few school leaders or advisers seem to appreciate that conflict and change went hand in hand because innovation inevitably challenged a teacher's existing values. Indeed many headteachers in the case studies appeared to back away from the consequences of these potential confrontations. As staff became more strongly committed to the innovation they would tend to challenge the position of colleagues who were slower to accept the new ideas. In order to reduce such tensions head teachers would often try to redirect the energies of the committed staff into 'safer' forms of non-controversial activity.

Similar reactions were described by teachers taking part in the ORACLE II project where innovation, whether it concerned introduction of new curriculum or a new teaching strategy within the school, appeared to be a rather haphazard procedure. One teacher, when interviewed, commented as follows:

Teacher	In maths particularly where the Head is trying and has been for some time to establish a standard way of teaching computation, everyone has a set of sheets as guidelines with a particular way of doing subtraction, multiplication and division, you know, that sort of thing.
Interviewer	Do you ever have whole school meetings where you talk about what you are doing across each subject areas?
Teacher	Yes. The Head calls staff meetings whenever he feels the need to discuss particular aspects of the curriculum with the whole staff. For example, if he is not happy about some aspect of maths then we will probably have a staff meeting where he will raise the point and we will discuss it.
Interviewer	Do you ever have meetings where you discuss how the content will be taught? If so, how do you decide on that 'how'?
Teacher	Yes. We have meetings like this and it's the head who decides the approach we will take. This is particularly the case in maths and he has got definite ideas about how we should teach it. So, at the meeting, he will say, 'I want you to use this approach'.
Interviewer	Is this approach successful in people having to change and do what the Head wants?
Teacher	I think it is too rosy a picture to say that at the moment. I think that he would like us to be doing it but I don't think though to be quite honest that we are doing anything like it.

While in another school the teacher reported that

> With the previous Head we didn't have any meetings to talk about curriculum changes and new approaches to teaching. It was very frustrating. Most of the staff we had at school started their teaching here and we didn't get any guidance on what we are supposed to be doing or where we were supposed to be going.

According to Kopmels (1989), however, without a clear organisational structure the school is unable to cope when such conflict arises. The Contact Schools' case studies showed that change had taken place in some schools despite the presence of teachers who were ineffective or reluctant to participate, despite unexpected events that had occurred during the process of school improvement and despite negative reactions from the local community. In order for the school to cope with these problems, Kopmels (1989: 488) argues that three conditions were necessary. First, there had to be clarity in the structure of organisation so that everyone was aware of the tasks that were expected of them. Second, there was a shared perception among participants of what was taking place within this organisational structure. While it was not necessary for all teachers to be involved in every decision, mechanisms were put in place which allowed individuals to be aware that such decisions were being considered. Third, and most important, there was consistency. The structures which existed between the school leader and the teachers supported the same kinds of practice which were advocated for the conduct of the relationship between the teacher and the children in the classroom.

It is this final recommendation that allows us to return once more to the main subject of this book, the development of collaboration between pupils in the classroom. In the course of the chapters we have endeavoured to set out a set of principles governing the development of such co-operative structures. Most importantly we have stressed that pupils need to understand why they are engaging in the processes of collaboration and also to be assured that the teacher understands what it *feels* like to have to work in this way. The same principles apply in the management of innovation. To be able to cope with the potential conflict and to develop the necessary commitment requires the same kind of collaborative structure. For this to happen teachers must be confident that the head teacher and the local authority adviser fully understand how it *feels*, as a participant in the classroom, to be part of such change.

There will be those who argue that the current climate, in which primary schools are fully preoccupied with the implementation of the National Curriculum, new schemes of assessment and the introduction of appraisal (trends which are seen not only in the United Kingdom but also in Australia and in other European countries), is unfavourable for the kinds of collaborative approaches suggested here. Those of us who believe that such approaches are commensurate with the aims of primary education – aims endorsed, for example, by the Member States of the Council of Europe (CDCC 1983 – must continue to believe that, over time, the political agenda for primary education will change. The introduction of the National Curriculum and the assessment schemes cannot obscure the fact that a fundamental problem within the primary school concerns the existing organisation which still demands that teachers simultaneously engage in a wide range of complex intellectual tasks with upwards of thirty over-dependent children. In such a situation careful assessment is extremely difficult and adequate monitoring well nigh impossible. The increase in collaborative group work, with its emphasis on inter-dependency between pupils, offers a practical solution to some of these more pressing problems and a sound basis for today's children as they prepare to face adult life in the twenty-first century.

REFERENCES

Abercrombie, M. L. (1960) *The Anatomy of Judgement: An Investigation into the Processes of Perception and Reasoning*, London: Hutchinson.

Abercrombie, M. L. (1970) *Aims and Techniques of Group Teaching*, Society for Research into Higher Education (SRHE working party on teaching methods, Publication 2), University of Surrey, Guildford.

Alexander, R. (1988) 'Garden or Jungle: Teachers' Development and Informal Primary Education', in Blythe, W. (ed) *Informal Primary Education Today: Essays and Studies*, London: Falmer Press.

Alexander, R., Willcocks, J. and Kinder, K. (1989) *Changing Primary Practice*, London: Falmer Press.

Anderson, L. and Burns, R. (1989) *Research in Classrooms: The Study of Teachers and Instruction*, Oxford: Pergamon.

Apple, M. (1979) *Ideology and Curriculum*, London: Routledge & Kegan Paul.

Armstrong, M. (1980) *Closely Observed Children: The Diary of a Primary Classroom*, London: Writers and Readers, Chameleon.

Armstrong, M. (1981) 'The Case of Louise and the Painting of Landscape', in Nixon, J. (ed) *A Teachers' Guide to Action Research*, London: Grant McIntyre.

Arnold, M. (1962) *Story Sequence Analysis*, New York: Columbia University Press.

Aronson, E. and Mills, J. (1959) 'The Effect of Severity of Initiation on Liking for a Group', *Journal of Abnormal and Social Psychology* 59, pp. 177–81.

Aronson, E., Blaney, N., Stephan, C., Sikes, J. and Snapp, M. (1978) *The Jig-saw Classroom*, London: Sage.

Ausubel, D. (1978) 'In Defense of Advanced Organisers: A Reply to the Critics', *Review of Educational Research* 48, pp. 251–7.

Bales, R. (1950) *Interaction Process Analysis: A Method of the Study of Small Groups*, Chicago: University of Chicago Press.

Bales, R. (1953) 'The Equilibrium Problem in Small Groups', in Parsons, T., Bales, R. and Shils, A. (eds) *Working Papers in the Theory of Action*, New York: Free Press.

Bales, R. and Cohen, S. (1979) *SYMLOG: A System for the Multiple Level Observation of Groups*, New York: Free Press.

Bandura, A. (1982) 'Self-efficacy Mechanism in Human Agency', *American Psychologist* 37 pp. 122–47.

Barker Lunn, J.C. (1970) *Streaming in the Primary School*, Slough: National Foundation for Educational Research.

Barnes, D. and Todd, F. (1977) *Communication and Learning in Small Groups*, London: Routledge & Kegan Paul.

Barnes, D., Britton, J. and Rosen, H. (1969) *Language, the Learner and the School*, Harmondworth: Penguin.

Bealing, D. (1972) 'Organization of Junior School Classroom', *Educational Research* 14, pp. 231–5.

Becker, H. S., Geer, B. and Hughes, E. (1968) *Making the Grade: The Academic Side of College Life*, New York: John Wiley.

Bellack, A. A., Hyman, R. T., Smith, F. L. and Kliebard, H. M. (1966) *The Language of the Classroom*, New York: Teachers' College Press, University of Columbia.

Bennett, N. (1985) 'Interaction and Achievement in Classroom Groups', in Bennett, N. and Desforges, C. (eds) *Recent Advances in Classroom Research*, *British Journal of Educational Psychology*, Monograph Series no. 2.

Bennett, N. and Blundell, D. (1983) 'Quality and Quality of Work in Rows and Classroom Groups', *Educational Psychology* 3 (2), pp. 93–105.

Bennett, N. and Cass, A. (1989) 'The Effects of Group Composition on Group Interactive Processes and Pupil Understanding', *British Educational Research Journal* 15 (1), pp 19–32.

Bennett, N. and Dunne, E. (1989) *Implementing Cooperative Groupwork in Classrooms*, Exeter: University of Exeter School of Education (Mimeograph).

Bennett, N., Desforges, C., Cockburn, A. and Wilkinson, B. (1984) *The Quality of Pupil Learning Experiences*, London: Lawrence Erlbaum.

Berlak, A. and Berlak, H. (1981) *Dilemmas of Schooling: Teaching and Social Change*, London: Methuen.

Berliner, D. (1986) 'Ways of Thinking about Students and Classrooms by More and Less Experienced Teachers', in Calderhead, J. (ed) *Exploring Teachers' Thinking*, London: Cassell.

Biott, C. (1987) 'Cooperative Group Work: Pupils' and Teachers' Membership and Participation', *Curriculum* 8 (2), pp. 5–14.

Blaney, N., Stephan, S., Rosenfield, D., Aronson, E. and Sikes, J. (1977) 'Interdependence in the Classroom: A Field Study', *Journal of Educational Psychology* 69, pp. 121–8.

Bloom, B. (1953) 'Thought Processes in Lectures and Discussions', *Journal of General Education* 7, pp. 160–9.

Bloom, B. (ed) (1956) *Taxonomy of Educational Objectives: The Classification of Educational Goals, Handbook 1: Cognitive Domain*, New York: McKay.

Boydell, D. (1975) 'Pupil Behaviour in Junior Classrooms', *British Journal of Educational Psychology* 45, pp. 122–9.

Brophy, J. and Good, T. (1986) 'Teacher Behaviour and Student Achievement', in Wittrock, M. (ed) *Handbook of Research on Teaching*, 3rd edition, New York: Macmillan.

Brown, R. (1988) *Group Processes: Dynamics Within and Between Groups*, Oxford: Basil Blackwell.

195

Burden, M., Emsley, M. and Constable, M. (1988) 'Encouraging Progress in Collaborative Group-work', *Education 3–13* 16 (1), pp. 51–6.

Burns, R. (1982) *Self Concept Development and Education*, London: Holt, Rinehart & Winston.

Burns, R. (1989) 'The Self Concept in Teacher Education', *South Pacific Journal of Teacher Education* 17 (2), pp. 27–38.

Calderhead, J. (1984) *Teachers' Classroom Decision Making*, London: Holt, Rinehart & Winston.

Campbell, D. and Stanley, J. (1963) 'Experimental and Quasi-Experimental Designs for Research on Teaching', in Gage, N. (ed) *Handbook of Research on Teaching*, Chicago: Rand McNally.

Carr, W. and Kemmis, S. (1986) *Becoming Critical: Education, Knowledge and Action Research*, London: Falmer Press.

Cavendish, S. J. (1988) 'Sex Differences Relating to Achievement in Mathematics', unpublished Ph.D. thesis, Leicester: University of Leicester.

Cavendish, S., Galton, M., Hargreaves, L. and Harlen, W. (1990) *Assessing Science in the Primary Classroom: Observing Activities*, London: Paul Chapman.

CDCC (Council for Cultural Cooperation) (1983) *Primary Education in Western Europe: Aims, Problems and Trends* DECS/EGT (83) 64, Strasbourg: Council of Europe

CDCC (Council for Cultural Cooperation) (1987) *Final Report: Project No. 8, Innovation in Primary Education in Europe* DECS/EGT (87) 23, Strasbourg: Council of Europe

Cohen, L. and Manion, L. (1980) *Research Methods in Education*, London: Croom Helm.

Cortazzi, M. (1990) *Primary Teaching: How it is, A Narrative Account*, London: David Fulton.

Cotton, J. and Cook, M. (1982) 'Meta Analysis and the Effect of Various Systems: Some Different Conclusions from Johnson et al.' *Psychological Bulletin* 92, pp. 176–83.

Covey, A. (1953) *Action Research to Improve School Practice*, New York: Teachers' College Press, University of Columbia.

Crozier, S. and Kleinberg, S. (1987) 'Solving Problems in a Group', *Education 3–13* 15 (3), pp. 37–41.

Cullingford, C. (1988) 'Children's Views about Working Together', *Education 3–13* 16 (1), pp. 29–34.

Day, J. (1983) 'The Zone of Proximal Development', in Pressley, M. and Levin, J. (eds) *Cognitive Strategy Research* no. 1, Springer Series in Cognitive Development, New York: Springer Verlag.

Deci, E. and Chandler, C. (1986) 'The Importance of Motivation for the Future of the L.D. Field', *Journal of Learning Disability* 19 (10), pp. 587–94.

Deci, E. and Ryan, R. (1985) *Intrinsic Motivation and Self Determination in Human Behaviour*, New York: Plenum Press.

Delamont, S. (1976) *Interaction in the Classroom*, 1st edition, London: Methuen.

Delamont, S. (1983) 'The Ethonography of Transfer', in Galton, M. and

Willcocks, J. (eds) *Moving from the Primary Classroom*, London: Routledge & Kegan Paul.

Department of Education and Science (1978) *Primary Education in England: A Survey by H.M. Inspectors of Schools*, London: HMSO.

Deutsch, M. (1949) 'An Experimental Study of the Effects of Cooperation and Competition upon Group Processes', *Human Relations* 2, pp. 199–231.

De Vries, D. and Slavin, R. (1978) 'Team-Games-Tournament (TGT): A Review of Ten Classroom Experiments', *Journal of Research and Development in Education* 12, pp. 28–38.

Doyle, W. (1983) 'Academic Work', *Review of Educational Research* 53 (2), pp. 159–99.

Doyle, W. (1986) 'Classroom Organisation and Management', in Wittrock, M. (ed) *Handbook of Research on Teaching*, 3rd edition, New York: Macmillan.

Doyle, W. and Ponder, G, (1977) 'The Practicality Ethic and Teacher Decision Making', *Interchange* 8, pp. 1–12.

Dunkin, M.J. and Biddle, B.J. (1974) *The Study of Teaching*, New York: Holt, Rinehart & Winston.

Dunne, E. and Bennett, N. (1990) *Talking and Learning in Groups*, London: Macmillan.

Edwards, A. and Westgate, D. (1987) *Investigating Classroom Talk*, Lewes: Falmer Press.

Elliott, J. (1976) *Developing Hypotheses about Classrooms from Teachers' Practical Constructs – An Account of the Work of the Ford Teaching Project*, North Dakota: North Dakota Study Group on Evaluation, University of North Dakota.

Elliott, J. (1978) 'Classroom Accountability and the Self-Monitoring Teacher', in Harlen, W. (ed) *Evaluation and the Teacher's Role*, Schools Council Research Studies, London: Macmillan Education.

Elliott, J, (1980) *Action-Research: A Framework for Self-Evaluation in Schools*, Working Paper No. 1 (mimeographed), Schools Council Programme 2, Teacher–pupil Interaction and the Quality of Learning Project, Cambridge: Cambridge Institute of Education.

Elliott, J. (1985) 'Facilitating Action Research in Schools: Some Dilemmas', in Burgess, R. (ed) *Field Methods in the Study of Education*, London: Falmer Press.

Elliott, J. (1989) 'Educational Theory and the Professional Learning of Teachers', *Cambridge Journal of Education* 19 (1), pp. 81–101.

Eraut, M. and Hoyles, C. (1989) 'Groupwork with Computers', *Journal of Computer Assisted Learning* 5 (1), pp. 12–24.

Fiedler, F., Chemers, M. and Makar, L. (1976) *Improving Leadership Effectiveness: The Leader Match Concept*, New York: John Wiley.

Fletcher, B. (1985) 'Group and Individual Learning of Junior School Children on a Microcomputer-based Task – Social or Cognitive Facilitation?', *Educational Review* 37 (3), pp. 251–61.

Forum observer (1966) 'The Junior School: Anatomy of the Non-streamed Classroom', *Forum* 8, pp. 79–85.

Fraser, B. (1986) *Classroom Environment*, London: Croom Helm.

French, J. (1990) 'Social Interaction in the Classroom', in Rogers, C. and

Kutnick, P. (eds) *The Social Psychology of the Primary School*, London: Routledge.

French, J. and French, P. (1984) 'Gender Imbalances in the Primary Classroom: An Interactional Account', *Educational Research* 26 (2), pp. 127–36.

Gage, N. (1985) *Hard Gains in the Soft Sciences: The Case of Pedagogy*, CEOR Monograph, Phi Delta Kappa, Bloomington, Indiana.

Galton, M. (1981) 'Teaching Groups in the Junior School: A Neglected Art', *Schools Organisation* 1 (2), pp. 175–81.

Galton, M. (1987) 'An ORACLE Chronicle: A Decade of Classroom Research', *Teaching and Teacher Education* 3 (4), pp. 229–314.

Galton, M. (1989) *Teaching in the Primary School*, London: David Fulton.

Galton, M. (1990) 'Primary Teacher Training: Practice in Search of a Pedagogy', in McClelland, A. and Varma, V. (eds) *Advances in Teacher Education*, London: Hodder & Stoughton.

Galton, M. and Blyth, W. (eds) (1989) *Handbook of Primary Education in Europe*, London: David Fulton.

Galton, M. and Patrick, H. (eds) (1990) *Curriculum Provision in Small Primary Schools*, London: Routledge.

Galton, M. and Willcocks, J. (eds) (1983) *Moving from the Primary Classroom*, London: Routledge & Kegan Paul.

Galton, M., Simon, B. and Croll, P. (1980) *Inside the Primary Classroom*, London: Routledge & Kegan Paul.

Glasser, W. (1986) *Control Theory in the Classroom*, New York: Harper & Row.

Glaye, A. (1986) 'Outer Appearances with Inner Experiences – Towards a More Holistic View of Group-Work', *Educational Review* 38 (1), pp. 45–56.

Goodlad, S. and Hirst, B. (1989) *Peer Tutoring: A Guide to Learning by Teaching*, London: Kogan Page.

Gordon, T. (1974) *T.E.T. Teacher Effectiveness Training*, New York: David Mckay.

Grundy, S. and Kemmis, S. (1981) 'Educational Action Research in Australia: The State of the Art', in *The Action Research Planner*, 1st edition, Geelong, Victoria: Deakin University Press.

Hertz-Lazarowitz, R. (1990) 'An Integrative Model of the Classroom: The Enhancement of Cooperation in Learning', Paper presented to the AERA annual meeting, Boston, April 1990, to be published in Hertz-Lazarowitz, R. and Miller, N. (eds) (in press) *Interaction in Cooperative Groups: Theoretical Anatomy of Group Learning*, London: Cambridge University Press.

Hertz-Lazarowitz, R. and Karsenty, G. (1990) 'Cooperative Learning and Student Achievement, Process Skills, Learning Environment and Self Esteem in 10th grade Biology classrooms', in Sharan, S. (ed) *Cooperative Learning: Research and Theory*, New York: Praeger.

Holt, J. (1984) *How Children Fail*, revised edition, Harmondsworth: Penguin.

Hord, S. (1987) *Evaluating Educational Innovation*, London: Croom Helm.

Hoyle, E. (1974) 'Professionality, Professionalism and Control in Teaching', *London Educational Review* 3 (2), pp. 13–19.

Hudson, L. (1966) *Frames of Mind*, London: Methuen.

Hustler, D., Cassidy, A. and Cuff, E.C. (eds) (1986) *Action Research in Classrooms and Schools*, London: Allen & Unwin.

Johnson, D. and Johnson, R. (1976) *Learning Together and Alone*, Englewood Cliffs, NJ: Prentice-Hall.

Johnson, D., Johnson, R., Johnson, J. and Anderson, D. (1976) 'Effects of Cooperative Versus Individualized Instruction on Student Presocial Behaviour, Attitudes towards Learning and Achievement', *Journal of Educational Psychology* 68, pp. 446–52.

Johnson, D., Johnson, R. and Scott, L. (1978) 'The Effects of Cooperative and Individualised Instruction on Student Attitudes and Achievement', *Journal of Social Psychology* 104, pp. 207–16.

Johnson, D., Johnson, R. and Skon, L. (1979) 'Student Achievement on Different Types of Tasks under Cooperative, Competitive and Individualistic Conditions', *Contemporary Educational Psychology* 4, pp. 99–106.

Johnson, D., Maruyama, G., Johnson, R., Nelson, D. and Shaw, L. (1981) 'Effects of Co-operative, Competitive and Individualistic goal structures in Achievement: A Meta Analysis', *Psychological Bulletin* 89, pp. 47–62.

Jones, D. (1988) 'Planning for Progressivism: The Changing Primary School in the Leicestershire Authority during the Mason Era 1947–71', in Lowe, R. (ed) *The Changing Primary School*, London: Falmer.

Joyce, B. and Showers, B. (1980) 'Improving In-Service Training: The Messages of Research', *Educational Leadership* 37 pp. 379–85.

Joyce, B. and Showers, B. (1983) 'Transfer of Training: the Contribution of Coaching', *Journal of Education* 163, (2), pp. 163–72.

Joyce, B. and Weil, M. (1986) *Models of Teaching*, 3rd edition, Englewood Cliffs, NJ: Prentice-Hall.

Kemmis, S. (1989) 'Improving Schools and Teaching through Educational Action Research', *Singapore Journal of Education*, Special Issue (Second Educational Research Association Annual Conference Papers).

Kerry, T. and Sands, M. (1982) *Handling Classroom Groups*, Nottingham: University of Nottingham School of Education (mimeo).

Koestner, R., Ryan, R., Bermen, F. and Holt, K. (1984) 'Setting Limits on Children's Behaviour: The Differential Effects of Controlling vs. Informational Styles on Intrinsic Motivation and Creativity', *Journal of Personality* 52 (3), pp. 233–48

Kopmels, D. (1987) *The Contact Schools Plan*, DECS/EGT (87) 34, Strasbourg: Council of Europe.

Kopmels, D. (1989) 'Innovation in Practice', in Galton, M. and Blyth, W. (eds) *Handbook of Primary Education in Europe*, London: David Fulton.

Kroath, F. (1989) 'How do Teachers change their Practical Theories?', *Cambridge Journal of Education* 19 (1), pp. 59–70.

Kutnick, P. (1988) *Relationships in the Primary School Classroom*, London: Paul Chapman.

Kutnick, P. (1990) 'Social Development of the Child and the Promotion of Autonomy in the Classroom', in Rogers, C. and Kutnick, P. (1990) *The Social Psychology of the Primary School*, London: Routledge.

Kyriacou, C. (1986) *Effective Teaching in Schools*, Oxford: Basil Blackwell.
Lucker, G., Rosenfield, D., Sikes, J. and Aronson, E. (1976) 'Performance in the Interdependent Classroom: A Field Study', *American Educational Research Journal* 13, pp. 115–23.
Lunzer, E. and Gardner, K. (eds) (1979) *The Effective Use of Reading*, Schools Council Project, London: Heinemann.
McClelland, D. (1963) 'On the Psychodynamics of Creative Physical Scientists', in Gruber, M. (ed) *Contemporary Approaches to Creative Thinking*, New York: Atherton.
McGlynn, R. (1982) 'A Comment on the Meta-Analysis of Goal Structures' *Psychological Bulletin* 92, pp. 184–5.
Measor, L. and Woods, P. (1984) *Changing Schools: Pupil Perspectives on Transfer to a Comprehensive*, Milton Keynes: Open University Press.
Moreland, R. and Levine, J. (1982) 'Socialisation in Small Groups: Temporal Changes in Individual–Group Relations', in Berkowitz, L. (ed) *Advances in Experimental Social Psychology*, vol. 15, New York: Academic Press.
Morgan, C. and Murray, M. (1935) 'A Method for Investigating Fantasies: The Thematic Apperception Test', *Archives of Neurology and Psychiatry* 34, pp. 289–294, reprinted in Semenoff, B. (ed) (1966) *Personality Assessment*, Harmondsworth: Penguin Modern Psychology Readings.
Mortimore, P., Sammons, P., Stoll, L.D. and Ecob, R. (1988) *School Matters: The Junior Years*, Wells: Open Books.
Nias, J. (1989) *Primary Teachers Talking*, London: Routledge.
Parlett, M. and Hamilton, D. (1976) 'Evaluation as Illumination', in Tawney, D. (ed) *Curriculum Evaluation Today: Trends and Implications*, Schools Council Research Series, London: Macmillan.
Piaget, J. (1959) *The Language and Thought of the Child*, London: Routledge & Kegan Paul.
Plowden Report (1967) *Children and their Primary Schools*, Report of the Central Advisory Council for Education in England (2 vols), London: HMSO.
Pollard, A. (1985) *The Social World of the Primary School*, London: Holt, Rinehart & Winston.
Pollard, A. (ed) (1987) *Children and their Primary Schools: A New Perspective*, London: Falmer Press.
Reid, J., Forrestal, P. and Cook, J. (1982) *Small Group Work in the Classroom*, Language and Learning Project – Education Department, Western Australia.
Richards, C. (1979) 'Primary Education; Myth, Belief and Practice', in Bloomer, M. and Shaw, K. (eds) *The Challenge of Educational Change*, Oxford: Pergamon.
Roeders, P. (1989) 'The Coaching Classroom: Increasing School Effectiveness by a Child Oriented, Creatively Based Educational Method', Paper given to 12th International School Psychology Association (ISPA) Conference, Ljublyana, August 1989.
Rosenbaum, M. E., Moore, D. L., Cotton, J. L., Cook, M. S., Hieser, R. A., Shover, M. N. and Gray, M. J. (1990) 'Group productivity and Processes:

Pure and Mixed Reward Structures and Task Interdependence', *Journal of Personality and Social Psychology* 39, pp. 626–42.

Rosenshine, B. and Furst, N. (1973) 'The Use of Direct Observation to Study Teaching', in Travers, R. (ed) *Second Handbook of Research on Teaching*, Chicago: Rand McNally.

Rowland, S. (1987) 'An Interpretative Model of Teaching and Learning', in Pollard, A. (ed) *Children and their Primary Schools*, London: Falmer Press.

Ryan, R., Connell, J. and Deci, E. (1985) 'A Motivational Analysis of Self-Determination and Self-Regulation in Education', in Ames, C. and Ames, R. (eds) *Research on Motivation in Education: The Classroom Milieu*, New York: Academic Press.

Sanford, R., Adkens, M., Miller, R. and Cobb, E. (1943) 'Physique, Personality and Scholarship', *Monograph of Society for Research into Child Development*, 8, no. 1.

Schunk, D. (1990) 'Self-Concept and School Achievement' in Rogers, C. and Kutnick, P. (eds) *The Social Psychology of the Primary School*, London: Routledge.

Sharan, S. (1980) 'Cooperative Learning in Small Groups: Recent Methods and Effects on Achievement, Attitudes and Ethnic Relations', *Review of Educational Research* 50, pp. 241–71.

Sharan, S., Kussell, P., Hertz-Lazarowitz, R., Bejarano, Y., Paviv, S. and Sharan, Y. (1984) *Cooperative Learning in the Classroom: Research in Desegregated Schools*, London: Lawrence Erlbaum.

Sinclair, J. and Coulthard, R. (1975) *Towards an Analysis of Discourse: The English Used by Teachers and Pupils*, Oxford: Oxford University Press.

Slavin, R. (1978) 'Student Teams and Achievement Divisions', *Journal of Research and Development in Education* 12, pp. 39–49.

Slavin, R. (1983a) *Co-operative Learning*, New York: Longman.

Slavin, R. (1983b) 'When does Cooperative Learning Increase Student Achievement?', *Psychological Bulletin* 94, pp. 429–45.

Slavin, R. (1986) 'Small Group Methods', in Dunkin, M. (ed) *The International Encyclopedia of Teaching and Teacher Education*, London: Pergamon.

Tann, S. (1981) 'Grouping and Group Work', in Simon, B. and Willcocks, J. (eds) *Research and Practice in the Primary Classroom*, London: Routledge & Kegan Paul.

Tizard, B., Blatchford, D., Burke, J., Farquhar, C. and Plewis, I. (1988) *Young Children at School in the Inner City*, Hove: Lawrence Erlbaum.

Tough (1977) *The Development of Meaning: A Study of Use of Language*, London: Allen & Unwin.

Turner, J. (1982) 'Towards a Cognitive Redefinition of the Social Group', in Tajfel, M. (ed) *Social Identity and Intergroup Relations*, Cambridge: Cambridge University Press.

Vygotsky, L. (1978) *Mind in Society: The Development of Higher Psychological Processes*, Cambridge, Mass: Harvard University Press.

Wallberg, H. and Anderson, G. (1968) 'Classroom Climate and Individual Learning', *Journal of Educational Psychology* 59, pp. 414–9.

Walker, C. (1974) *Reading Development and Extension*, London: Ward Lock.

Warren, N, and Jahoda, M. (eds) (1976) *Attitudes: Selected Readings*, Harmondsworth: Penguin.

Webb, N. (1983) 'Predicting Learning from Student Interaction: Defining the Interaction Variables', *Educational Psychologist* 18 (1), pp. 33–41.

Webb, N. (1985) 'Verbal Interaction and Learning in Peer Directed Groups', *Theory into Practice* 24 (1), pp. 32–9.

Webb, N. (1989) 'Peer Interaction and Learning in Small Groups', *International Journal of Educational Research* 13, pp. 21–39.

Weiner, B. (1986) *Attributional Theory of Motivation and Emotion*, New York: Springer-Verlag.

Wells, L. and Maxwell, G. (1976) *Self Esteem: its Measurement and Conceptualisation*, Beverly Hills, Calif: Sage.

Wheldall, K., Morris, M., Vaughan, P. and Yin Yuk No (1981) 'Rows v Tables: An Example of the Use of Behavioural Ecology in Two Classes of Eleven Year Old Children', *Educational Psychology* 1 (2), pp. 171–83.

Williamson, J. (1988) 'Working with Teachers', unpublished Ph.D. thesis, University of Leicester.

Wittrock, M. (1986) (ed) *Handbook of Research on Teaching*, 3rd Edition, New York: Macmillan.

Wood, D. (1988) *How Children Think and Learn*, Oxford: Basil Blackwell.

Yeomans, A. (1983) 'Collaborative Group Work in Primary and Secondary Schools: Britain and the USA', *Durham and Newcastle Research Review* X (51), pp. 99–105.

INDEX